Anonymous

The Catholic Hymnal.

Hymns Selected for Public and Private Use

Anonymous

The Catholic Hymnal.
Hymns Selected for Public and Private Use

ISBN/EAN: 9783744657341

Printed in Europe, USA, Canada, Australia, Japan

Cover: Foto ©Lupo / pixelio.de

More available books at **www.hansebooks.com**

The Catholic Hymnal.

HYMNS

SELECTED FOR PUBLIC AND PRIVATE USE.

LONDON:
BURNS & LAMBERT, 17 PORTMAN STREET,
AND 63 PATERNOSTER ROW.

LONDON:
PRINTED BY ROBSON, LEVEY, AND FRANKLYN,
Great New Street and Fetter Lane.

The hymns in this Hymnal are arranged on a plan different from that ordinarily in use. They are arranged in the following order: first, the hymns to God, the Ever-blessed Trinity; then those which relate to the Mysteries of the Incarnation, and its consequences; our Lord's twofold Parentage; the Sacrifice of the Mass; and the Blessed Sacrament. After these follow hymns relating to Himself and His mystical Body. Thus we come to hymns for His Sacred Heart, and Precious Blood and Passion. Then to hymns for our Blessed Lady's Festivals; and after these, to hymns for Festivals of the Holy Angels and Saints, and for the different Seasons of the Church. At the end there is a number of miscellaneous hymns, chiefly relating to the interior life. Some of these are intended for private reading.

Most of the hymns in this Hymnal are already well known, as Father Faber and Father Caswall have kindly permitted the selection to be made from their writings; that is, principally from the *Oratory Hymn-book* and *Catholic Hymns* by Father Faber, and from *Translations of the Breviary Hymns* and *The Masque of Mary and other Poems* by Father Caswall.

It is hoped that this arrangement may in some measure supply the want long felt for a more complete and varied Hymnal.

INDEX OF HYMNS

FOR THE PRINCIPAL FEASTS AND ECCLESIASTICAL SEASONS.

Advent, 78, 79, 80.
Christmas, 26, 81, 82, 83, 84, 120, 175, 181.
Lent, 86, 87, 88, 89.
The Passion, 14, 27, 28, 29, 32, 33, 36, 37, 38, 39, 40, 41, 42, 43, 44; 45, 46, 161, 169.
Easter, 90, 91, 92, 93, 94.
Ascension, 15, 95, 96, 97, 98.
Pentecost, 4, 5, 6, 99, 100, 101, 103.
Holy Trinity, 1, 7, 8.
Corpus Christi, 16, 17, 18, 19, 20, 22, 102, 104, 105, 176.
Sacred Heart, 23, 24, 174.
B.V.M., 31, 83, 47 to 77, 177.
St. Joseph, 116, 178.
Apostles, 110, 111, 112, 113, 114, 115, 121, 122, 123.
Saints' days, 117, 118, 119, 124, 125, 126, 127, 128, 129, 130, 131, 132, 173.
Holy Angels, 106, 107, 108, 109.

HYMNS.

1. Almighty God.

1 My God, how wonderful Thou art!
   Thy Majesty how bright!
How beautiful Thy Mercy-Seat
   In depths of burning light!

2 How dread are Thine eternal years,
   O everlasting Lord!
By prostrate spirits day and night
   Unceasingly adored.

3 Oh, how I fear Thee, Living God!
   With deepest, tenderest fears,
And worship Thee with trembling hope
   And penitential tears.

4 Yet I may love Thee, too, O Lord!
   Almighty as Thou art;
For Thou hast stooped to ask of me
   The love of my poor heart.

5 Oh, then this worse than worthless heart
   In pity deign to take,
And make it love Thee for Thyself,
   And for Thy glory's sake.

6 No earthly father loves like Thee;
   No mother half so mild
Bears and forbears, as Thou hast done
   With me Thy sinful child.

7 Only to sit and think of God,
   Oh, what a joy it is!
To think the thought, to breathe the Name,
   Earth has no higher bliss!

8 Father of Jesus! love's Reward!
   What rapture will it be
Prostrate before Thy throne to lie,
   And gaze and gaze on Thee!

---

2.   My Father.

1 O GOD! Thy power is wonderful,
   Thy glory passing bright;
Thy wisdom, with its deep on deep,
   A rapture to the sight.

2 Thy justice is the gladdest thing
   Creation can behold;
Thy tenderness so meek, it wins
   The guilty to be bold.

3 Yet more than all, and ever more,
   Should we Thy creatures bless,
Most worshipful of attributes,
   Thine awful holiness.

4 Angelic spirits, countless souls,
   Of Thee have drunk their fill;
And to eternity will drink
   Thy joy and glory still.

5 Mary, herself a sea of grace,
    Hath all been drawn from Thine;
  And Thou couldst fill a thousand more
    From out those depths divine.

6 From Thee were drawn those worlds of life,
    The Saviour's Heart and Soul;
  And undiminished still Thy waves
    Of calmest glory roll.

7 All things that have been, all that are,
    All things that can be dreamed,
  All possible creations, made,
    Kept faithful, or redeemed;—

8 Oh, little heart of mine! shall pain
    Or sorrow make thee moan,
  When all this God is all for thee,
    A Father all thine own?

---

3. Jesus, my God and my all.

1 O Jesus, Jesus! dearest Lord!
    Forgive me if I say
  For very love Thy sacred Name
    A thousand times a day.

2 I love Thee so, I know not how
    My transports to control;
  Thy love is like a burning fire
    Within my very soul.

3 Oh, wonderful! that Thou shouldst let
    So vile a heart as mine
  Love Thee with such a love as this,
    And make so free with Thine.

4 The craft of this wise world of ours
   Poor wisdom seems to me;
Ah! dearest Jesus! I have grown
   Childish with love of Thee.

5 For Thou to me art all in all,
   My honour and my wealth,
My heart's desire, my body's strength,
   My soul's eternal health.

6 O Light in darkness, Joy in grief,
   O Heaven begun on earth!
Jesus! my Love! my Treasure! who
   Can tell what Thou art worth?

7 O Jesus, Jesus! sweetest Lord!
   What art Thou not to me?
Each hour brings joys before unknown,
   Each day new liberty!

8 O love of Jesus! Blessed love!
   So will it ever be;
Time cannot hold Thy wondrous growth,
   No, nor eternity.

4.   Veni Creator.

1 COME, Holy Ghost, Creator, come!
The darkness of our minds illume;
Thy children's hearts, O God, inspire,
And lighten with celestial fire.

2 Thou that art named the Paraclete,
The Gift of God, His Spirit sweet;
The Living Fountain, Fire, and Love,
And gracious Unction from above:

3 Of God's Right Hand the Finger Thou,
  Who dost Thy sevenfold grace bestow;
  True promise of the Father, rich
  In gifts of tongues and various speech.

4 Enable with perpetual light
  The dullness of our blinded sight;
  Our hearts with heavenly love fulfil
  To walk Thy way, and do Thy will.

5 Stablish our weakness, and refresh
  With fortitude our fainting flesh:
  Keep far our foes, give peace at home:
  Where Thou art guide no ill can come.

6 Teach us to know the Father, Son,
  And Thee, of both, to be but One,
  That through the ages all along
  This faith may be love's endless song.

7 To God the Father laud and praise,
  And to the Son, whom He did raise,
  And to the Holy Spirit be,
  Now and for all eternity.

5. Veni Sancte Spiritus.

1 COME, Holy Spirit! from the height
  Of Heaven send down Thy blessed light!
    Come, Father of the friendless poor!
  Giver of gifts, and light of hearts,
  Come with that unction which imparts
    Such consolations as endure.

2 The Soul's Refreshment and her Guest,
  Shelter in heat, in labour Rest,

The sweetest Solace in our woe!
Come, blissful Light! oh, come and fill
In all Thy faithful, heart and will,
   And make our inward fervour glow.

3 Where Thou art, Lord! there is no ill,
For evil's self Thy light can kill:
   Oh, let that light upon us rise!
Lord, heal our wounds and cleanse our stains,
Fountain of grace! and with Thy rains
   Our barren spirits fertilise.

4 Bend with Thy fires our stubborn will,
And quicken what the world would chill,
   And homeward call the feet that stray:
Virtue's reward, and final grace,
The Eternal Vision face to face,—
   Spirit of Love! for these we pray.

5 Come, Holy Spirit! bid us live;
To those who trust Thy mercy give
   Joys that through endless ages flow:
Thy various gifts, foretastes of Heaven,
Those that are named Thy Sacred Seven,
   On us, O God of love! bestow.

6. Holy Ghost, come down upon Thy Children.

1 HOLY GHOST, come down upon Thy children,
   Give us grace, and make us Thine;
Thy tender fires within us kindle,
   Blessed Spirit! Dove Divine!
For all within us good and holy
   Is from Thee, Thy precious gift;
In all our joys, in all our sorrows,
   Wistful hearts to Thee we lift.
      Holy Ghost, &c.

2 For Thou to us art more than father,
   More than sister, in Thy love,
 So gentle, patient, and forbearing,
   Holy Spirit, Heavenly Dove!
     Holy Ghost, &c.

3 Oh, we have grieved Thee, gracious Spirit!
   Wayward, wanton, cold are we;
 And still our sins, new every morning,
   Never yet have wearied Thee.
     Holy Ghost, &c.

4 Dear Paraclete! how hast thou waited
   While our hearts were slowly turned!
 How often hath Thy love been slighted,
   While for us it grieved and burned!
     Holy Ghost, &c.

5 Now, if our hearts do not deceive us,
   We would take Thee for our Lord;
 Oh, dearest Spirit! make us faithful
   To Thy least and lightest word.
     Holy Ghost, &c.

6 Ah! sweet Consoler, though we cannot
   Love Thee as Thou lovest us;
 Yet if Thou deign'st our hearts to kindle,
   They will not be always thus.
     Holy Ghost, &c.

7 With hearts so vile how dare we venture,
   King of kings, to love Thee so?
 And how canst Thou, with such compassion,
   Bear so long with things so low?
     Holy Ghost, &c.

7. Hymn to the Most Holy Trinity.

1 O Thou immortal Light divine!
   Dread Trinity in Unity!
Almighty One! Almighty Trine!
   Give ear to Thy creation's cry.

2 Father! in majesty enthron'd!
   Thee we confess with Thy dear Son;
Thee, Holy Ghost! eternal Bond
   Of love,—uniting Both in One.

3 As from the Father increate,
   His Son and Word eternal came;
So, too, from Each the Paraclete
   Proceeds, in Deity the same;

4 Three Persons!—among whom is none
   Greater in majesty or less;
In substance, essence, nature, One;
   Equal in might and holiness.

5 Three Persons, One Immensity,
   Encircling utmost space and time!
One Greatness, Glory, Sanctity,
   One everlasting Truth sublime!

6 O Lord, most holy, wise, and just!
   Author of nature! God of grace!
Grant that as now in Thee we trust,
   So we may see Thee face to face.

7 Thou art the Fount of all that is;
   Thou art our origin and end;
On Thee alone our future bliss
   And perpetuity depend.

8 Thou solely didst the worlds create,
   Subsisting still by Thy decree;
Thou art the light, the glory great,
   And prize of all who hope in Thee!

9 To Father, Son, and Holy Ghost,
    Triunal Lord of earth and Heaven!
From earth and from the heavenly host
    Be sempiternal glory given!

---

8. The Most Holy Trinity.

1 HAVE mercy on us, God Most High!
    Who lift our hearts to Thee;
Have mercy on us worms of earth,
    Most Holy Trinity!

2 Most ancient of all mysteries!
    Before Thy throne we lie;
Have mercy now, most merciful,
    Most Holy Trinity!

3 When Heaven and earth were yet unmade,
    When time was yet unknown,
Thou in Thy bliss and majesty
    Didst live and love alone!

4 Thou wert not born, there was no fount
    From which Thy Being flowed;
There is no end which Thou canst reach:
    But Thou art simply God.

5 Oh, listen, then, Most Pitiful!
    To Thy poor creature's heart;
It blesses Thee that Thou art God,
    That Thou art what Thou art!

6 Most ancient of all mysteries!
    Still at Thy throne we lie!
Have mercy now, most merciful,

9. Hymn to the Most Holy Will of God.

1 SOVEREIGN Will enthroned on high,
    In th' Eternal's awful breast,
Thee we laud and glorify,
    Ever perfect, ever best.

2 Order, wisdom, beauty, might,
    Sanctity, and love are Thine;
Truth Thy sempiternal light,
    Equity Thy law divine.

3 Thee the heav'ns adore and bless;
    Thee, wherever worlds extend,
All created things confess
    Their beginning as their end.

4 Thee the fallen sons of men
    Their eternal glory own;
Call'd to Paradise again
    By Thy purest grace alone.

5 Oh, confirm our feeble will
    All Thy counsels to obey;
Where it hears Thy whisper still,
    There to press without delay.

6 Glory to the Godhead trine,
    Only true and only fair!
One in will and pow'r divine,
    One in providential care!

Christ's Humanity.

1 IT is my sweetest comfort, Lord,
    And will for ever be,
To muse upon the gracious truth
    Of Thy humanity.

2 O joy! there sitteth in our flesh,
  Upon a throne of light,
 One of a human mother born,
  In blazing Godhead bright!

3 Though earth's foundations should be mov'd
  Down to their lowest deep;
 Though all the trembling universe
  Into destruction sweep,—

4 For ever God, for ever man,
  My Jesus shall endure;
 And fix'd on Him, my hope remains
  Eternally secure.

11. Christ's Twofold Parentage.

1 CHRIST has two Parents, in a twofold scheme,
  A twofold birth sublime;
 A Father, from eternity supreme,
  A Mother, born in time.

2 He from His Father, by a termless birth,
  Without a Mother came;
 Created highest Heav'n, this lower earth,
  And all the starry frame.

3 He from His Mother, in the midst of years,
  Without a Father born,
 Drain'd to the dregs the chalice of our tears,
  Then died in pain and scorn.

4 O peerless mystery of depth and height,
  In one same Person seen!
 O finite closely knit with Infinite!
  Celestial with terrene!

5 Jesu, by Thy eternal Father's might,
    Hear Thou my trembling prayer:
Thou who art God of God, and Light of Light,
    Omnipotent to spare!

6 Jesu, by Thy sweet Mother's tender love,
    Look tenderly on me;
Remember, mighty as Thou art above,
    I am one flesh with Thee!

12.   2.

1 HAIL, dread Paternity, whereby
    The unbegotten Lord,
Before eternal years, begot
    His co-eternal Word!

2 And hail, thou sweet Maternity!
    Whereby, O love sublime,
That same eternal Word for us
    Was born again in time!

3 Oh, Father, by thy Son made man,
    Hear Thou our trembling cry!
Oh, Mother, by thy Babe divine,
    Plead thou for us on high!

4 Jesu, by Thy dread Father's might,
    By Thy sweet Mother's name,
Upon Thy human brethren shed
    Thy Spirit's holy flame.

13.   3.

1 ETERNAL Glory of the heav'ns!
    Blest Hope of all on earth!
God, of eternal Godhead born!
    Man, by a virgin birth!

2 Jesu, true Sun of human souls!
  Shed in our souls Thy ray;
 And with Thy touch our lips inspire
  Their meed of praise to pay.

3 Steep all our senses in Thy beam;
  The world's false night expel;
 Purge each defilement from our breasts,
  And there for ever dwell.

4 Thou who dost grant th' accepted time,
  Give tears to purify;
 Give fire of love to burn our hearts
  As victims unto Thee.

14. Christ our High-Priest and Sacrifice.

1 SING, O earth, for thy redemption!
  Lo, His race of torment run,
 Christ the Sanctuary enters,
  Priest and Victim both in one;
 There to make our peace with God,
 By th' Oblation of His blood!

2 Guilty for the guilty pleading,
  Legal Priest, Thy task is o'er!
 Goats and oxen,—empty shadows,—
  There is need of you no more!
 Not such feeble things as these
 Could an' angry God appease!

3 Hail to Thee, High-Priest eternal;
  Priest without a spot of sin;
 Veil'd of old in mystic figures;
  Holy, infinite, divine!
 Thou art He whose Blood alone
 Can for human guilt atone!

4 Thou of life the Lord Anointed,
   Led to Thy self-chosen doom,
That same Flesh which Thou hadst moulded
   In Thy Virgin Mother's womb
Offerest on the Holy Rood ;
Man for man, and God to God !

5 While the rage of Thy tormentors,
   In its very fury blind,
As from Thy pure veins it madly
   Pours the ransom of mankind,
Does but work Thy own decree,
Fix'd from all eternity !

---

15. Christ's Session at the Right Hand of God.

1 Soon the fiery sun ascending
   Will have chas'd the midnight gloom;—
Rise, O Thou High-Priest eternal;
   Break the bondage of the tomb ;
And above the vaulted sky
Bear Thy victim Flesh on high !

2 Once on earth for guilty mortals
   Sacrific'd in torment sore,
There may it, on Heav'n's high altar,
   Plead our cause for evermore;
And appease an injur'd God,
With the Lamb's atoning Blood.

3 Nam'd of old High-Priest for ever,
   By the Father's stedfast oath,
Rise, O Advocate Almighty,
   Rise, O Priest and Victim both !
Swiftly, swiftly speed Thy way
Back to golden realms of day.

4 Lo, 'tis done! O'er death victorious
    Christ ascends His starry throne;
There from all His labours resting
    Still He travails for His own;
Still our fate His Heart employs
E'en amid eternal joys.

5 There He sits in tranquil glory;
    There He stands His aid to lend;
There He offers to His Father
    Every single prayer we send;
There Himself receives each sigh
As omniscient Deity!

---

16. The Most Holy Sacrifice of the Mass.

1 WHEN the Patriarch was returning
    Crown'd with triumph from the fray,
Him the peaceful king of Salem
    Came to meet upon his way;
Meekly bearing Bread and Wine,
Holy Priesthood's awful sign!

2 On the truth thus dimly shadow'd,
    Later days a lustre shed;
When the great High-Priest eternal,
    Under forms of Wine and Bread,
For the world's immortal food
Gave His Flesh and gave His Blood.

3 Wondrous gift!—The Word who moulded
    All things by His might divine,
Bread into His Body changes,
    Into his own Blood the wine:
What though sense no change perceives,
Faith admires, adores, believes!

4 He who once to die a Victim
   On the Cross did not refuse,
Day by day upon our altars
   That same Sacrifice renews;
Through His holy Priesthood's hands
Faithful to His last commands!

5 While the people all uniting
   In the Sacrifice sublime
Offer Christ to His high Father,
   Offer up themselves with Him,
Then together with the Priest
On the living Victim feast!

17. The Blessed Sacrament.

1 Hail, Thou living Bread from Heaven!
   Sacrament of awful might!
I adore Thee,—I adore Thee,—
   Every moment, day and night.

2 Holiest Jesu!—Heart of Mary!
   O'er me shed your gifts divine:
Holiest Jesu! my Redeemer!
   All my heart and soul are Thine.

18.   2.

1 O Jesu Christ, remember,
   When Thou shalt come again,
Upon the clouds of Heaven,
   With all thy shining train;—

2 When every eye shall see Thee
  In Deity reveal'd,
Who now upon this altar
  In silence art conceal'd;—

3 Remember then, O Saviour,
  I supplicate of Thee,
That here I bow'd before Thee
  Upon my bended knee ;

4 That here I own'd Thy Presence,
  And did not Thee deny;
And glorified Thy greatness,
  Though hid from human eye.

5 Accept, divine Redeemer,
  The homage of my praise;
Be Thou the light and honour
  And glory of my days.

6 Be Thou my consolation
  When death is drawing nigh;
Be Thou my only treasure
  Through all eternity.

19.   3.

1 O GODHEAD hid, devoutly I adore Thee,
Who truly art within the forms before me ;
To Thee my heart I bow with bended knee,
As failing quite in contemplating Thee.

2 Sight, touch, and taste in Thee are each deceived ;
The ear alone most safely is believ'd:
I believe all the Son of God has spoken,

3 God only on the Cross lay hid from view;
But here lies hid at once the Manhood too:
And I, in both professing my belief,
Make the same prayer as the repentant thief.

4 Thy wounds, as Thomas saw, I do not see;
Yet Thee confess my Lord and God to be:
Make me believe Thee ever more and more;
In Thee my hope, in Thee my love to store.

5 O thou Memorial of our Lord's own dying!
O living Bread, to mortals life supplying!
Make Thou my soul henceforth on Thee to live;
Ever a taste of Heavenly sweetness give.

6 Jesu! whom for the present veil'd I see,
What I so thirst for, oh, vouchsafe to me:
That I may see Thy countenance unfolding,
And may be blest Thy glory in beholding.

[*The following is usually sung after every stanza.*]

Jesu, eternal Shepherd! hear our cry;
Increase the faith of all whose souls on Thee rely.

---

20.   4.

1 HAIL to Thee! true Body sprung
From the Virgin Mary's womb!
The same that on the Cross was hung,
And bore for man the bitter doom!

2 Thou, whose side was pierced, and flow'd
Both with water and with blood;
Suffer us to taste of Thee,
In our life's last agony.

3 O kind, O loving One!
O sweet Jesu, Mary's Son!

21. The Transfiguration of Our Lord Jesus Christ.

1 ALL ye who seek, in hope and love,
 For your dear Lord, look up above!
 Where, trac'd upon the azure sky,
 Faith may a glorious form descry.

2 Lo! on the trembling verge of light
 A something all divinely bright!
 Immortal, infinite, sublime!
 Older than chaos, space, or time!

3 Hail, Thou, the Gentiles' mighty Lord
 All hail, O Israel's King ador'd!
 To Abraham sworn in ages past,
 And to his seed while earth shall last.

4 To Thee the prophets witness bear;
 Of Thee the Father doth declare,
 That all who would His glory see,
 Must hear and must believe in Thee.

5 To Jesus, from the proud conceal'd,
 But evermore to babes reveal'd,
 All glory with the Father be,
 And Holy Ghost, eternally.

22. The Divine Word.

1 THE Word, descending from above,
  Though with the Father still on high,
 Went forth upon His work of love,
  And soon to life's last eve drew nigh.

2 He shortly to a death accurs'd
  By a disciple shall be given;
 But, to His twelve disciples, first
  He gives Himself, the Bread from Heaven.

3 Himself in either kind He gave;
   He gave His Flesh, He gave His Blood;
Of flesh and blood all men are made;
   And He of man would be the Food.

4 At birth, our brother He became;
   At board, Himself as food He gives;
To ransom us He died in shame;
   As our reward, in bliss He lives.

5 O saving Victim! opening wide
   The gate of Heav'n to man below!
Our foes press on from every side;—
   Thine aid supply, thy strength bestow.

6 To thy great Name be endless praise,
   Immortal Godhead, One in Three!
Oh, grant us endless length of days,
   In our true native land, with Thee!

23. The most Sacred Heart of Jesus.

1 JESU, Creator of the world!
   Of all mankind Redeemer blest!
True God of God! in whom we see
   The Father's Image clear express'd!

2 Thee, Saviour, love alone constrain'd
   To make our mortal flesh thine own;
And as a second Adam come,
   For the first Adam to atone.

3 That self-same love, which made the sky,
   Which made the sea, and stars, and earth
Took pity on our misery,
   And broke the bondage of our birth.

4 O Jesu! in thy heart divine
    May that same love for ever glow;
For ever mercy to mankind
    From that exhaustless fountain flow.

5 For this thy sacred heart was pierc'd,
    And both with blood and water ran;
To cleanse us from the stains of guilt,
    And be the hope and strength of man.

6 To God the Father, and the Son,
    All praise, and power, and glory be;
With Thee, O holy Comforter,
    Henceforth through all eternity.

24.   2.

1 ALL ye who seek a certain cure
    In trouble and distress,
Whatever sorrow vex the mind,
    Or guilt the soul oppress:

2 Jesus, who gave Himself for you
    Upon the Cross to die,
Opens to you His sacred Heart,—
    Oh, to that Heart draw nigh!

3 Ye hear how kindly He invites;
    Ye hear His words so blest;—
"All ye that labour, come to Me,
    And I will give you rest."

4 What meeker than the Saviour's Heart?—
    As on the Cross He lay,
It did his murderers forgive,
    And for their pardon pray.

5 O Heart! thou joy of Saints on high!
    Thou Hope of sinners here!
  Attracted by those loving words,
    To Thee I lift my prayer.

6 Wash Thou my wounds in that dear Blood
    Which forth from Thee doth flow;
  New grace, new hope inspire; a new
    And better heart bestow.

---

25.   The Holy Name.

1 Jesu! the very thought of Thee
    With sweetness fills my breast;
  But sweeter far Thy face to see,
    And in Thy presence rest.

2 Nor voice can sing, nor heart can frame,
    Nor can the memory find,
  A sweeter sound than Thy blest name,
    O Saviour of mankind!

3 O hope of every contrite heart,
    O joy of all the meek,
  To those who fall how kind Thou art!
    How good to those who seek!

4 But what to those who find? ah! this
    Nor tongue nor pen can show:
  The love of Jesus, what it is,
    None but His lov'd ones know.

5 Jesu! our only joy be Thou,
    As Thou our prize wilt be;
  Jesu! be Thou our glory now
    And through eternity.

Part II.

1 O Jesu! King most wonderful!
    Thou Conqueror renown'd,
  Thou Sweetness most ineffable,
    In whom all joys are found!

2 When once Thou visitest the heart,
    Then truth begins to shine;
  Then earthly vanities depart;
    Then kindles love divine.

3 O Jesu! Light of all below!
    Thou Fount of life and fire!
  Surpassing all the joys we know,
    And all we can desire:

4 May every heart confess Thy name,
    And ever Thee adore;
  And, seeking Thee, itself inflame
    To seek Thee more and more.

5 Thee may our tongues for ever bless,
    Thee may we love alone;
  And ever in our lives express
    The image of Thine own.

Part III.

1 O Jesu! Thou the beauty art
    Of angel worlds above:
  Thy Name is music to the heart,
    Enchanting it with love.

2 Celestial sweetness unalloy'd!
    Who eat Thee hunger still!
  Who drink of Thee still feel a void,
    Which nought but Thou canst fill.

3 Oh, my sweet Jesu! hear the sighs
    Which unto Thee I send;
  To Thee mine inmost spirit cries,
    My being's hope and end!

4 Stay with us, Lord, and with Thy light
    Illume the soul's abyss;
Scatter the darkness of our night,
    And fill the world with bliss.

5 O Jesu! spotless Virgin flower!
    Our life and joy! to Thee
Be praise, beatitude, and power,
    Through all eternity.

26. Hymn to the Infant Jesus.

1   Sleep, holy Babe,
    Upon Thy Mother's breast;
The Lord of earth, and sea, and sky,
How sweet it is to see Thee lie
    In such a place of rest!

2   Sleep, holy Babe,
    Thine angels watch around,
All bending low with folded wings,
Before the Incarnate King of kings,
    In reverent awe profound.

3   Sleep, holy Babe,
    While I with Mary gaze
In joy upon that face awhile,
Upon the beatific smile
    Which there divinely plays.

4   Sleep, holy Babe,
    Oh, snatch Thy brief repose;
Too quickly will Thy slumber break,
And Thou to lengthen'd pains awake,
    Which death alone shall close.

5 Then must those hands
Which now so small I see,
Those feet so lovely and divine,
That flesh so delicately fine,
 Be pierced and rent for me!

6 Then must that brow
Its thorny crown receive;
That cheek which now so roseate glows
Be drench'd with blood, and marr'd with blows,
 That I thereby may live!

7 O Lady Blest!
To thee I suppliant cry;
Forgive the wrong that I have done,
In causing by my sins thy Son
 Upon the Cross to die.

8 O Jesu Lord!
By Thy sweet childhood's years,
Blot out from their terrific page
My sins of youth and later age,
 In these my contrite tears.

9 So may I sing
Immortal praise to Thee,
Who, once a Babe of human birth,
Now reignest Lord of heaven and earth,
 Through all eternity.

27. The Precious Blood.

1 HAIL, Jesus! hail! who for my sake
 Sweet Blood from Mary's veins didst take,
  And shed it all for me;
O blessed be my Saviour's Blood,
My life, my light, my only good,
  To all eternity.

2 To endless ages let us praise
  The Precious Blood, whose price could raise
    The world from wrath and sin;
  Whose streams our inward thirst appease,
  And heal the sinner's worst disease,
    If he but bathe therein.

3 O sweetest Blood, that can implore
  Pardon of God, and heaven restore,
    The heaven which sin had lost:
  While Abel's blood for vengeance pleads,
  What Jesus shed still intercedes
    For those who wrong Him most.

4 Oh, to be sprinkled from the wells
  Of Christ's own sacred Blood excels
    Earth's best and highest bliss;
  The ministers of wrath divine
  Hurt not the happy hearts that shine
    With those red drops of His!

5 Ah! there is joy amid the Saints,
  And hell's despairing courage faints
    When this sweet song we raise:
  Oh, louder then, and louder still,
  Earth with one mighty chorus fill,
    The Precious Blood to praise!

---

28.   The Agony.

1 O SOUL of Jesus, sick to death!
  Thy blood and prayer together plead!
  My sins have bowed Thee to the ground,
  As the storm bows the feeble reed.

2 Deep waters have come in, O Lord!
All darkly on thy Human Soul;
And clouds of supernatural gloom
Around Thee are allowed to roll.

3 The weight of the eternal wrath
Drives over Thee with pressure dread:
And forced upon the olive-roots,
In death-like sadness droops Thy Head.

4 Thy Spirit weighs the sins of men;
Thy science fathoms all their guilt;
Thou sick'nest heavily at Thy Heart,
And the pores open,—blood is spilt.

5 And Thou hast shuddered at each act,
And shrunk with an astonished fear,
As if Thou couldst not bear to see
The loathsomeness of sin so near.

Part II.

1 My God! my God! and can it be
That I should sin so lightly now,
And think no more of evil thoughts
Than of the wind that waves the bough?

2 I sin, and heaven and earth go round,
As if no dreadful deed were done,
As if God's Blood had never flowed
To hinder sin, or to atone.

3 I walk the earth with lightsome step,
Smile at the sunshine, breathe the air,
Do my own will, nor ever heed
Gethsemane and Thy long prayer.

4 Shall it be always thus, O Lord?
Wilt Thou not work this hour in me
The grace Thy Passion merited,
Hatred of self and love of Thee?

5 Oh, by the pains of thy pure love,
　Grant me the gift of holy fear;
　And give me of Thy Bloody Sweat
　To wash my guilty conscience clear!

6 And make me feel it was my sin,
　As though no other sins there were,
　That was to Him who bears the world
　A load that He could scarcely bear!

---

29.   Jesus crucified.

1 Oh, come and mourn with me awhile;
　See, Mary calls us to her side;
　Oh, come and let us mourn with her:
　Jesus, our Love, is crucified!

2 Have we no tears to shed for Him,
　While soldiers scoff and Jews deride?
　Ah, look how patiently He hangs:
　Jesus, our Love, is crucified!

3 Seven times He spoke, seven words of love,
　And all three hours His silence cried
　For mercy on the souls of men:
　Jesus, our Love, is crucified!

4 Come, take thy stand beneath the Cross,
　And let the Blood from out that Side
　Fall gently on thee drop by drop:
　Jesus, our Love, is crucified!

5 A broken heart, a fount of tears,
　Ask, and they will not be denied;
　A broken heart love's cradle is:
　Jesus, our Love, is crucified!

6 O Love of God! O Sin of man!
  In this dread act your strength is tried;
  And victory remains with love,
  For He, our Love, is crucified!

---

30. The Descent of Jesus to Limbus.

1 THOUSANDS of years had come and gone,
    And slow the ages seemed to move
  To those expectant souls that filled
    That prison-house of patient love.

2 It was a weary watch of theirs,
    But onward still their hopes would press;
  Captives they were, yet happy too
    In their contented weariness.

3 Sweet tidings there St. Joseph took;
    The Saviour's work had then begun,
  And of His three-and-thirty years
    But three alone were left to run.

4 And Eve, like Joseph's shadow, hung
    About him wheresoe'er he went;
  She lived on thoughts of Mary's child,
    Trembled with hope, and was content.

5 But see! how hushed the crowd of souls!
    Whence comes the light of upper day?
  What glorious Form is this that finds
    Through central earth its ready way?

6 'Tis God! 'tis Man! the living Soul
    Of Jesus, beautiful and bright,
  The first-born of created things,
    Flushed with a pure resplendent light.

7 'Twas Mary's child! Eve saw Him come;
   She flew from Joseph's haunted side,
And worshiped, first of all that crowd,
   The Soul of Jesus crucified.

8 So after four long thousand years,
   Faith reached her end, and Hope her aim;
And from them, as they passed away,
   Love lit her everlasting flame.

31. The Seven Dolours of the Blessed Virgin Mary.

1 WHAT a sea of tears and sorrow
   Did the soul of Mary toss
To and fro upon its billows,
   While she wept her bitter loss;
In her arms her Jesus holding,
   Torn but newly from the Cross!

4 Oh, that mournful Virgin Mother!
   See her tears how fast they flow
Down upon His mangled body,
   Wounded side, and thorny brow;
While his hands and feet she kisses,
   Picture of immortal woe!

3 Oft and oft His arms and bosom
   Fondly straining to her own;
Oft her pallid lips imprinting
   On each wound of her dear Son;
Till at last, in swoons of anguish,
   Sense and consciousness are gone.

4 Gentle Mother, we beseech thee,
    By thy tears and trouble sore;
By the death of thy dear Offspring;
    By the bloody wounds He bore;
Touch our hearts with that true sorrow
    Which afflicted thee of yore.

5 To the Father everlasting,
    And the Son, who reigns on high,
With the coeternal Spirit,
    Trinity in Unity,
Be salvation, honour, blessing,
    Now and through eternity.

32.   2.

1 Come, darkness, spread o'er heav'n thy pall,
    And hide, O sun, thy face;
While we that bitter death recall,
    With all its dire disgrace.

2 And thou, with tearful cheek, wast there;
    But with a heart of steel,
Mary, thou didst His moanings hear,
    And all His torments feel.

3 He hung before thee crucified;
    His flesh with scourgings rent;
His bloody gashes gaping wide;
    His strength and spirit spent.

4 Thou His dishonour'd countenance,
    And racking thirst, didst see;
By turns the gall, the sponge, the lance,
    Were agony to thee.

5 Yet still erect in majesty,
 Thou didst the sight sustain;—
Oh, more than Martyr! not to die
 Amid such cruel pain!

6 Praise to the blessed Three in One;
 Oh, may that strength be mine,
Which, sorrowing o'er her only Son,
 Did in the Virgin shine.

33.   3.

1 AT the cross her station keeping,
Stood the mournful Mother weeping, *Cas:*
 Close to Jesus to the last:
Through her heart His sorrow sharing,
All His bitter anguish bearing,
 Lo, the piercing sword hath passed.

2 Oh, how sad and sore distressèd,
Now was she, that Mother blessèd *Mant*
 Of the sole-begotten One;
Woe-begone, with heart's prostration,
Mother meek, the bitter passion
 Saw she of her glorious Son.

3 Who could mark, from tears refraining,
Christ's dear Mother uncomplaining,
 In so great a sorrow bow'd?
Who unmov'd behold her languish
Underneath His Cross of anguish,
 'Mid the fierce unpitying crowd?

4 In His people's sins rejected, *Mant*
She her Jesus, unprotected,
 Saw with thorns, with scourges rent:
Saw her Son from judgment taken,
Her belov'd in death forsaken,
 Till His spirit forth He sent.

5 Fount of Love and holy sorrow,
   Mother! may my spirit borrow
     Somewhat of thy woe profound
   Unto Christ, with pure emotion,
   Raise my contrite heart's devotion,
     Love to read in every wound.

6 Those five Wounds of Jesu smitten,
   Mother! in my heart be written,
     Deep as in thine own they be:
   Thou, my Saviour's Cross who bearest,
   Thou, thy Son's rebuke who sharest,
     Let me share them both with thee.

7 In the Passion of my Maker
   Be my sinful soul partaker,
     Weep till death, and weep with thee;
   Mine with thee be that sad station,
   There to watch the great salvation
     Wrought upon th' atoning Tree.

8 When in death my limbs are failing,
   Let Thy Mother's prayer prevailing
     Lift me, Jesu! to Thy throne:
   To my parting soul be given
   Entrance through the gate of heaven;
     There confess me for Thine own.

---

34.   4.

1 HOLY Mother! pierce me through:
   In my heart each wound renew
     Of my Saviour crucified:
   Let me share with thee His pain,
   Who for all my sins was slain,
     Who for me in torments died.

2 Let me mingle tears with thee,
  Mourning Him who mourn'd for me,
    All the days that I may live:
  By the Cross with thee to stay,
  There with thee to weep and pray,
    Is all I ask of thee to give.

35. 5.

1 VIRGIN of all virgins best!
  Listen to my fond request:
    Let me share thy grief divine;
  Let me, to my latest breath,
  In my body bear the death
    Of that dying Son of thine.

2 Wounded with His every wound,
  Steep my soul till it hath swoon'd
    In His very blood away;
  Be to me, O Virgin, nigh,
  Lest in flames I burn and die,
    In His awful Judgment-day.

3 Christ, when Thou shalt call me hence,
  Be Thy Mother my defence,
    Be Thy Cross my victory;
  While my body here decays,
  May my soul Thy goodness praise,
    Safe in Paradise with Thee.

36. Prayer of our Lord Jesus Christ on Mount Olivet.

1 SEE from on high, array'd in truth and grace,
    The Father's Word descend!
  Burning to heal the wounds of Adam's race,
    And our long evils end!

2 Pitying the miseries which with the Fall
  In Paradise began,
 Prostrate upon the earth, the Lord of all
  Entreats for ruin'd man.

3 Oh, bitter then was our Redeemer's lot,
  While whelm'd in griefs unknown:
 " Father," He cries, " remove this cup ; yet not
  My will, but Thine be done."

4 While, a dread anguish pressing down His heart,
  He faints upon the ground ;
 And from each bursting pore the blood-drops start,
  Moistening the earth around.

5 But quickly, from high Heav'n, an angel came,
  To soothe the Saviour's woes ;
 And, strength returning to his languid frame,
  Up from the earth He rose.

6 Praise to the Father; praise, O Son, to Thee,
  To whom a name is given
 Above all names; praise to the Spirit be,
  From all in earth and heaven.

37.   2.

1 DAUGHTER of Sion! cease thy bitter tears,
  And calm thy breast ;
 Foretold through ages past, lo! now appears
  Thy Mediator blest.

2 That garden, where of old our guilt began,
  Wrought death and pain;
 But this, where Jesus prays by night for man,
  Brings life and joy again.

3 Hither, of His own will, the Lord for all
    Comes to atone;
And stays the thunderbolts about to fall
    From the dread Father's throne.

4 So shall He break the adamantine chain
    Of Hell's abyss;
And opening Heav'n long clos'd, call us again
    To His eternal bliss.

5 Praise to the Son, to whom a name above
    All names is given;
Praise to the Father and the Spirit of love,
    From all in earth and Heaven.

38. The Passion of our Lord.

1 SEE! where in shame the God of glory hangs,
    All bath'd in His own blood:
See! how the nails pierce with a thousand pangs
    Those hands so good.

2 Th' All Holy, as a minister of ill,
    Betwixt two thieves they place;
Oh, deed unjust! yet such the cruel will
    Of Israel's race.

3 Pale grows His face, and fix'd His languid eye;
    His wearied head He bends;
And rich in merits, forth with one loud cry
    His Spirit sends.

4 Oh, heart more hard than iron! not to weep
    At this; thy sin it was
That wrought His death; of all these torments deep
    Thou art the cause.

5 Praise, honour, glory be through endless time
    To th' everlasting God,
Who wip'd away our deadly stains of crime
    In His own Blood.

---

39.   2.

1 O'ERWHELM'D in depths of woe,
    Upon the Tree of scorn
Hangs the Redeemer of mankind,
    With racking anguish torn.

2 See! how the nails those hands
    And feet so tender rend;
See! down His face, and neck, and breast,
    His sacred Blood descend.

3 Hark! with what awful cry
    His Spirit takes its flight;
That cry, it pierc'd His Mother's heart,
    And whelm'd her soul in night.

4 Earth hears, and to its base
    Rocks wildly to and fro;
Tombs burst; seas, rivers, mountains quake;
    The veil is rent in two.

5 The sun withdraws his light;
    The midday heav'ns grow pale;
The moon, the stars, the universe,
    Their Maker's death bewail.

6 Shall man alone be mute?
    Come, youth! and hoary hairs!
Come, rich and poor! come, all mankind!
    And bathe those feet in tears.

7 Come, fall before His Cross,
    Who shed for us His blood;
  Who died the victim of pure love,
    To make us sons of God.

8 Jesu! all praise to Thee,
    Our joy and endless rest!
  Be Thou our guide while pilgrims here,
    Our crown amid the blest!

---

40.   3.

1 FORTH comes the Standard of the King:
    All hail, thou Mystery ador'd!
  Hail, Cross! on which the Life Himself
    Died, and by death our life restor'd.

2 On which our Saviour's holy side,
    Rent open with a cruel spear,
  Of blood and water pour'd a stream,
    To wash us from defilement clear.

3 O sacred Wood! in thee fulfill'd
    Was holy David's truthful lay;
  Which told the world, that from a Tree
    The Lord should all the nations sway.

4 Most royally empurpled o'er,
    How beauteously thy stem doth shine!
  How glorious was its lot to touch
    Those limbs so holy and divine!

5 Thrice blest, upon whose arms outstretch'd
    The Saviour of the world reclin'd;
  Balance sublime! upon whose beam
    Was weigh'd the ransom of mankind.

6 Hail, Cross! thou only hope of man,
    Hail on this holy Passion-day!
  To saints increase the grace they have;
    From sinners purge their guilt away.

7 Salvation's spring, blest Trinity,
    Be praise to Thee through earth and skies:
  Thou through the Cross the victory
    Dost give; oh, also give the prize!

41. The Most Holy Crown of Thorns of our Lord Jesus Christ.

1 DAUGHTERS of Sion! royal maids!
    Come forth to see the crown,
  Which Sion's self, with cruel hands,
    Hath woven for her Son.

2 See! how amid His gory locks
    The jagged thorns appear;
  See! how His pallid countenance
    Foretells that death is near.

3 Oh, savage was the earth that bore
    Those thorns so sharp and long!
  Savage the hand that gather'd them
    To work this deadly wrong!

4 But now that Christ's immortal Blood
    Hath ting'd them with its dye,
  Fairer than roses they appear,
    Or palms of victory.

5 Jesu! the thorns which pierc'd Thy brow
    Sprang from the seed of sin;
  Pluck ours, we pray Thee, from our hearts,
    And plant thine own therein.

42. The Spear and Nails of our Lord Jesus Christ.

1 Hail, Spear and Nails! erewhile despis'd,
 As things of little worth;
Now crimson with the blood of Christ,
 And fam'd through Heav'n and earth.

2 Chosen by Jewish perfidy
 As instruments of sin,
God turn'd you into ministers
 Of love and grace divine:

3 For from each several wound ye made
 In that immortal frame,
As from a fount, celestial gifts
 And life eternal came.

4 Thee, Jesu, pierc'd with Nails and Spear,
 Let every knee adore;
With Thee, O Father, and with Thee,
 O Spirit, evermore.

Part II.

1 Oh, turn those blessed points, all bath'd
 In Jesu's blood, on me;
Mine were the sins that wrought His death,
 Mine be the penalty.

2 Pierce through my feet, my hands, my heart;
 So may some drop distil
Of Blood divine, into my soul,
 And all its evils heal.

3 So shall my feet be slow to sin,
 Harmless my hands shall be;
So from my wounded heart shall each
 Forbidden passion flee.

4 Thee, Jesu, pierc'd with Nails and Spear,
   Let every knee adore;
With Thee, O Father, and with Thee,
   O Spirit, evermore.

43. The Most Holy Winding-Sheet of our Lord Jesus Christ.

1 THIS day the wond'rous mystery
   Is set before our eyes,
Of Jesus stretch'd upon the Cross
   In dying agonies.

2 Oh, deed of love! the Prince becomes
   A Victim for His slave;
The sinner an acquittal finds,
   The innocent a grave.

3 Whereof, in many a gory stain,
   The traces still are found
On yonder Winding-Sheet, which wrapp'd
   The sacred body round.

4 Hail, trophies of our valiant Chief!
   Hail, proofs of triumph won
Over the World, and Hell, and Death,
   By God's eternal Son!

5 Be these the colours under which
   From this time forth we fight,
Against the depths of Satan's guile,
   And all the powers of night.

6 So, dead to our old life, may we
   A better life begin;
And through the Cross of Christ at length
   His Heavenly Crown attain.

44. The Most Precious Blood of our Lord Jesus Christ.

1 Forth let the long procession stream,
   And through the streets in order wend;
Let the bright waving line of torches gleam,
   The solemn chant ascend.

2 While we, with tears and sighs profound,
   That memorable Blood record,
Which, stretch'd on His hard Cross, from many a wound
   The dying Jesus pour'd.

3 By the first Adam's fatal sin
   Came death upon the human race;
In this new Adam doth new life begin,
   And everlasting grace.

4 For scarce the Father heard from Heaven
   The cry of His expiring Son,
When in that cry our sins were all forgiven,
   And boundless pardon won.

5 Henceforth, whoso in that dear Blood
   Washeth, shall lose his every stain;
And in immortal roseate beauty rob'd,
   An angel's likeness gain.

6 Only, run thou with courage on
   Straight to the goal set in the skies;
He, who assists thy course, will give thee soon
   The everlasting prize.

7 Father supreme! vouchsafe that we,
   For whom Thine only Son was slain,
And whom Thy Holy Ghost dost sanctify,
   May heavenly joys attain.

45. 2.

1 HE who once, in righteous vengeance,
    Whelm'd the world beneath the flood,
Once again in mercy cleans'd it
    With the stream of His own Blood,
Coming from His throne on high
On the painful Cross to die.

2 Oh, the wisdom of th' Eternal!
    Oh, its depth, and height divine!
Oh, the sweetness of that mercy
    Which in Jesus Christ doth shine!
The guilty slave was doom'd to die—
The Just One pays the penalty.

3 When before the Judge we tremble,
    Conscious of His broken laws,
May this Blood, in that dread hour,
    Cry aloud, and plead our cause:
Bid our guilty terrors cease,
Be our pardon and our peace.

4 Prince and Author of salvation!
    Lord of majesty supreme!
Jesu! praise to Thee be given
    By the world Thou didst redeem;
Who, with the Father, and the Spirit,
Reignest in eternal merit.

46. The Five Sacred Wounds.

1 Hail, Wounds! which through eternal years
    The love of Jesus show;
Hail, Wounds! from whence encrimson'd rills
    Of blood for ever flow.

2 How doth th' ensanguin'd thorny crown
    That beauteous brow transpierce!
How do the nails those hands and feet
    Contract with tortures fierce!

3 He bows His head, and forth at last
    His loving spirit soars;
Yet even after death His heart
    For us its tribute pours.

4 Oh, come all ye in whom are fix'd
    The deadly stains of sin!
Come! wash in this all-saving Blood,
    And ye shall be made clean.

5 Praise Him, who with the Father sits
    Enthron'd upon the skies;
Whose Blood redeems our souls from guilt,
    Whose Spirit sanctifies.

HYMNS

TO THE BLESSED VIRGIN.

47. **From the First Sunday in Advent to the Feast of the Purification.**

MOTHER of Christ! hear thou thy people's cry,
Star of the deep, and Portal of the sky!
Mother of Him who thee from nothing made,
Sinking we strive, and call to thee for aid:
Oh, by that joy which Gabriel brought to thee,
Thou Virgin first and last, let us thy mercy see.

From the Purification of the Blessed Virgin to Palm-Sunday.

HAIL, O Queen of Heav'n enthroned!
Hail, by angels Mistress own'd!
Root of Jesse! Gate of morn!
Whence the world's true Light was born:
Glorious Virgin, joy to thee,
Loveliest whom in Heaven they see:
Fairest thou where all are fair!
Plead with Christ our sins to spare.

From Easter-Sunday to Whit-Sunday.

Joy to thee, O Queen of Heaven! Alleluia.
  He whom thou wast meet to bear; Alleluia.
As He promised, hath arisen; Alleluia.
  Pour for us to Him thy prayer; Alleluia.

From Trinity-Sunday to the Last Sunday after Pentecost.

Mother of mercy, hail, O gentle Queen!
Our life, our sweetness, and our hope, all hail!
    Children of Eve,
To thee we cry from our sad banishment,
    To thee we send our sighs,
Weeping and mourning in this tearful vale.
    Come, then, our Advocate;
Oh, turn on us those pitying eyes of thine:
    And our long exile past,
      Show us at last
Jesus, of thy pure womb the fruit divine.
  O Virgin Mary, mother blest!
  O sweetest, gentlest, holiest!

---

48. The Immaculate Conception.

Part I.

1 O purest of creatures! sweet Mother! sweet Maid!
The one spotless womb wherein Jesus was laid!
Dark night hath come down on us, Mother! and we
Look out for thy shining, sweet Star of the Sea!

2 Deep night hath come down on this rough-spoken world,
And the banners of darkness are boldly unfurled;
And the tempest-tossed Church, all her eyes are on thee,
They look to thy shining, sweet Star of the Sea.

3 The Church doth what God had first taught her
   to do;
 He looked o'er the world to find hearts that were
   true;
 Through the ages He looked, and He found none
   but thee,
 And He loved thy clear shining, sweet Star of
   the Sea!

4 He gazed on thy soul: it was spotless and fair;
 For the empire of sin, it had never been there;
 None had e'er owned thee, dear Mother! but
   He,
 And He blessed thy clear shining, sweet Star of
   the Sea!

5 Earth gave Him one lodging: 'twas deep in thy
   breast,
 And God found a home where the sinner finds
   rest;
 His home and His hiding-place, both were in
   thee,
 He was won by thy shining, sweet Star of the
   Sea!

6 Oh, blissful and calm was the wonderful rest
 That thou gavest thy God in thy virginal breast;
 For the heaven He left, He found heaven in
   thee,
 And He shone in thy shining, sweet Star of the
   Sea!

Part II.

7 To sinners what comfort, to angels what mirth,
 That God found one creature unfallen on earth,
 One spot where His Spirit untroubled could be,
 The depths of thy shining, sweet Star of the
   Sea!

8 So age after age in the Church had gone round,
   And the Saints new inventions of homage have found,
   New titles of honour, new honours for thee,
   New love for thy shining, sweet Star of the Sea!

9 And now from the Church of all lands thy dear name
   Comes borne on the breath of one mighty acclaim;
   Men call on their father that he should decree
   A new gem to thy shining, sweet Star of the Sea!

10 Oh, shine on us brighter than ever, then, shine!
   For the primest of honours, dear Mother! is thine;
   "Conceived without sin," thy new title shall be,
   Clear light from thy birth-spring, sweet Star of the Sea!

11 So worship we God in these rude latter days;
   So worship we Jesus, our Love, when we praise
   His wonderful grace in the gifts He gave thee—
   The gift of clear shining, sweet Star of the Sea!

12 Deep night hath come down on us, Mother! deep night,
   And we need more than ever the guide of thy light;
   For the darker the night is, the brighter should be
   Thy beautiful shining, sweet Star of the Sea!

49.   2.

1 The day, the happy day, is dawning,
  The glorious feast of Mary's chiefest praise,
 That brightens, like a second morning,
  The clouded evening of these latter days.
   O every clime! O every nation!
   Praise, praise the God of our salvation!

2 High up, the realm of angels ringeth
  With hymns of triumph to its mortal queen,
 While earth its song of welcome singeth
  In every shady grove and valley green.
   O every clime! &c.

3 Hail, Queen, whose life is just beginning,
  Thrice welcome, Mother of a fallen race,
 The sinless come to save the sinning,
  Thyself the chosen aqueduct of grace.
   O every clime! &c.

4 Immaculate! O dear exemption,
  A spotless soul for God, entire and free.
 Redeemed with such a choice redemption,
  Angel nor saint can share the praise with thee.
   O every clime! &c.

5 O Virgin brighter than the brightest
  'Mid all the beauteous throngs that shine above!
 O maiden whiter than the whitest
  Of lily-flowers in Eden's sacred grove!
   O every clime! &c.

6 Chief miracle of God's compassion,
  Choice mirror of His burning holiness,
 Whose heart His mercy deigned to fashion
  Far more than Eva's ruin to redress.
   O every clime! &c.

7 See! Mary comes! O jubilation!
    She comes with love to cheer a guilty race;
 O triumph! triumph, all creation;
    O Christians! triumph in redeeming grace.
      O every clime! &c.

---

50. Our Lady's Presentation.

1 Day breaks on temple-roofs and towers;
  The city sleeps, the palms are still;
  The fairest far of earth's fair flowers
     Mounts Sion's sacred hill.

2 O wondrous Babe! O Child of grace!
  The Holy Trinity's delight!
  Sweetly renewing man's lost race,
     How fair thou art, how bright!

3 Not all the vast angelic choirs,
  That worship round the eternal throne,
  With all their love can match the fires
     Of thy one heart alone.

4 Since God created land and sea,
  No love hath been so like divine;
  For none was ever like to thee,
     Nor worship like to thine.

5 Angels in heaven, and souls on earth,
  Thousands of years their songs may raise,
  Nor equal thee, for thine was worth
     All their united praise.

6 O Maiden most immaculate!
  Make me to choose thy better part;
  And give my Lord, with love as great,
  An undivided heart.

7 Would that my heart, dear Lord! were true,
Royal and undefiled and whole,
Like hers from whom Thy sweet love took
   The Blood to save my soul.

8 If here our hearts grudge aught to Thee,—
In that bright land beyond the grave
We'll worship Thee with souls set free,
   And give as Mary gave.

51. Our Lady's Expectation.

1 Like the dawning of the morning
   On the mountain's golden heights,
Like the breaking of the moonbeams
   On the gloom of cloudy nights,
Like a secret told by angels
   Getting known upon the earth,
Is the Mother's Expectation
   Of Messiah's speedy birth!

2 Thou wert happy, blessed Mother!
   With the very bliss of heaven,
Since the angel's salutation
   In thy raptured ear was given;
Since the Ave of that midnight
   When thou wert anointed Queen,
Like a river overflowing
   Hath the grace within thee been.

3 On the mountains of Judæa,
   Like the chariot of the Lord,
Thou wert lifted in thy spirit
   By the uncreated Word;
Gifts and graces flowed upon thee
   In a sweet celestial strife,
And the growing of thy Burden
   Was the lightening of thy life.

4 And what wonders have been in thee
　　All the day and all the night,
　While the Angels fell before thee,
　　To adore the Light of Light.
　While the glory of the Father
　　Hath been in thee as a home,
　And the sceptre of creation
　　Hath been wielded in thy womb.

5 Thou hast waited, Child of David!
　　And thy waiting now is o'er!
　Thou hast seen Him, Blessed Mother!
　　And wilt see Him evermore!
　Oh, His Human Face and Features,
　　They were passing sweet to see:
　Thou beholdest them this moment;
　　Mother, show them now to me!

52. The Purification.

1 Joy! joy! the Mother comes,
　　And in her arms she brings
　The Light of all the world,
　　The Christ, the King of kings;
　And in her heart the while
　　All silently she sings.

2 St. Joseph follows near,
　　In rapture lost and love,
　While angels round about
　　In glowing circles move,
　And o'er the Mother broods
　　The Everlasting Dove.

3 There in the Temple-court
　　Old Simeon's heart beats high,

And Anna feeds her soul
  With food of prophecy;
But, see! the shadows pass,
  The world's true Light draws nigh.

4 O Infant God! O Christ!
    O Light most beautiful!
  Thou comest, Joy of joys!
    All darkness to annul;
  And brightest lights of earth
    Beside Thy Light are dull.

5 Ah! with what thrills of awe
    The Mother's heart is teeming,
  To think the new-born Light,
    That o'er the world is streaming,
  At His own Mother's hands
    Should stoop to need redeeming!

6 Then to that Mother now
    All rightful worship be!
  For Thou hast ransomed Him
    Who first did ransom Thee;
  Oh, with thy Mother's tongue
    Pray Him to ransom me!

---

53. The Dolours of our Lady.

1 God of Mercy! let us run
    Where yon fount of sorrows flows;
  Pondering sweetly, one by one,
    Jesu's wounds and Mary's woes.

2 Ah! those tears Our Lady shed,
    Enough to drown a world of sin;
  Tears that Jesu's sorrows fed,
    Peace and pardon well may win!

3 His five Wounds a very home
    For our prayers and praises prove;
And our Lady's Woes become
    Endless joys in Heaven above.

4 Jesus, who for us didst die,
    All on Thee our love we pour;
And, in the Holy Trinity,
    Worship Thee for evermore.

54.   The Assumption.

1 SING, sing, ye Angel Bands,
    All beautiful and bright;
For higher still, and higher,
    Through fields of starry light,
Mary, your Queen, ascends,
    Like the sweet moon at night.

2 A fairer flower than she
    On earth hath never been;
And, save the Throne of God,
    Your heavens have never seen
A wonder half so bright
    As your ascending Queen.

3 O happy Angels! look,
    How beautiful she is!
See! Jesus bears her up,
    Her hand is locked in His;
Oh, who can tell the height
    Of that fair Mother's bliss?

4 And shall I lose thee then,
    Lose my sweet right to thee?
Ah, no! the Angels' Queen
    Man's mother still will be;
And thou, upon thy throne,
    Wilt keep thy love for me.

5 On, through the countless stars
    Proceeds the bright array;
And Love Divine comes forth
    To light her on her way,
Through the short gloom of night
    Into celestial day.

6 Swifter and swifter grows
    That marvellous flight of love,
As though her heart were drawn
    More vehemently above;
While jubilant angels part
    A pathway for the Dove!

7 Hark! hark! through highest heaven
    What sounds of mystic mirth!
Mary, by God proclaimed
    Queen of Immaculate Birth,
And diademed with stars,
    The lowliest of the earth!

8 See! see! the Eternal Hands
    Put on her radiant crown,
And the sweet Majesty
    Of Mercy sitteth down,
For ever and for ever,
    On her predestined throne!

55.   To our Blessed Lady.

1 MOTHER of Mercy! day by day
   My love of thee grows more and more;
Thy gifts are strewn upon my way
   Like sands upon the great sea-shore.

2 Though poverty and work and woe
   The masters of my life may be,
When times are worst, who does not know
   Darkness is light with love of thee?

3 But scornful men have coldly said
   Thy love was leading me from God;
And yet in this I did but tread
   The very path my Saviour trod.

4 They know but little of thy worth
   Who speak these heartless words to me;
For what did Jesus love on earth
   One half so tenderly as thee?

5 Get me the grace to love thee more;
   Jesus will give, if thou wilt plead;
And, Mother! when life's cares are o'er,
   Oh, I shall love thee then indeed!

6 Jesus, when His three hours were run,
   Bequeath'd thee from the cross to me;
And oh! how can I love thy Son,
   Sweet Mother! if I love not thee?

---

56.   2.

1 HAIL, Mary, only sinless child
   Of guilty Adam's fallen race;
Conceiv'd all pure and undefil'd,
   Through thy dear Lord's preventing grace.

2 He would not have the blight of sin
   A moment rest thy soul upon;
For pure without, and pure within,
   Must be the Mother of His Son.

3 No haughty fiend might boast that he
   One moment held thee in his snare,
Who of the dread Divinity
   Wert destin'd for the Temple fair.

4 Thus wert thou sinless in thy birth,
   And sinless after as before;
The only creature of this earth
   Whom sin ne'er cast its shadow o'er.

5 O sweetest lily! all untorn,
   Though nurs'd the thorns of earth among,
To thee we sigh, to thee we mourn,
   To thee we lift our suppliant song.

6 From Satan's snare preserve us free,
   And keep us safe from earthly stain,
That in this world we pure may be,
   And in the next may see thee reign.

---

57. Mary, our Mother, reigns on high.

1 O VISION bright!
   The land of light
Beams goldenly beyond the sky;
   'Mid heavenly fires,
   'Bove angel-choirs,
Mary, our Mother, reigns on high.

2 O vision bright!
   The Father's might

All round His daughter's throne doth lie;
   Where, in the balm
   Of endless calm,
Mary, our Mother, reigns on high.

  3 O vision bright!
   The eternal light
Of the dear Son may we descry;
   Where, brighter far
   Than moon or star,
Mary, our Mother, reigns on high.

  4 O vision bright!
   In softest flight
The Dove around His Spouse doth fly;
   Where, in that height
   Of matchless light,
Mary, our Mother, reigns on high.

  5 O vision bright!
   Angels' delight!
The Mother sits with Jesus nigh:
   Her form He bears,
   Her look He wears;
Mary, our Mother, reigns on high.

  6 O vision bright!
   O dearest sight!
God, with His Mother's face and eye!
   Where by His side,
   All glorified,
Mary, our Mother, reigns on high.

  7 O vision bright!
   Life's darkest night
Is fair as dawn when thou art nigh;
   Where, 'mid the throng
   Of psalm and song,
Mary, our Mother, reigns on high.

8 O vision bright!
 O land of light!
Thou art our home beyond the sky;
 'Tis grand to see
 How gloriously
Mary, our Mother, reigns on high.

---

58. 5.

1 STAR of Jacob, ever beaming
  With a radiance all divine!
 'Mid the stars of highest heaven
  Glows no purer ray than thine.

2 All in stoles of snowy brightness,
  Unto thee the angels sing;
 Unto thee the virgin choirs,—
  Mother of th' eternal King!

3 Joyful in thy path they scatter
  Roses white and lilies fair;
 Yet with thy chaste bosom's whiteness
  Rose nor lily may compare.

4 Oh, that this low earth of ours,
  Answering th' angelic strain,
 With thy praises might reëcho
  Till the heavens replied again.

5 Honour, glory, virtue, merit,
  Be to Thee, O Virgin's Son!
 With the Father and the Spirit,
  While eternal ages run.

59. 6.

1 ALL hail, O Lady of the world,
  The Queen of heaven most high;
Thou peerless Virgin, radiant Star
  That lights the morning sky.

2 All hail, thou full of every grace,
  And bright with light divine;
Oh, speed, sweet Lady, to the world,
  Come with thy help benign.

3 For thee of old the Lord ordain'd
  From all eternity,
Ev'n of his sole-begotten Word
  The Mother bright to be;

4 Of Him who made earth, sea, and sky,
  And deck'd thee out all fair,
His perfect bride, that thou mightst have
  In Adam's guilt no share.

60. 7.

1 HAIL, Virgin-flower! hail, mother-maid!
  Untainted,—free from blame;
Hail, Queen of Mercy, who dost wear
  The starry diadem.

2 More pure and more immaculate
  Than purest angels are,
Thou standest at the King's right hand
  In golden raiment fair.

3 Through thee, O Mother of all grace,
  The sinner's hope most sure,
The star that lights the dang'rous sea,
  The port of rest secure,

4 The ever-open gate of Heaven,
　　Health of each soul that faints,—
　Through thee may we behold the King
　　In mansions of the saints.

61.　　　　8.

1 THE moon is in the heavens above,
　　And its light lies on the foamy sea;
　So shines the star of Mary's love
　　O'er this stormy scene of misery.
　Our hands to life's hard work are laid,
　　But our hearts are thine,
　　　　Sweet Mother-Maid!

2 Oh, thou art bright as bright can be,
　　And as bountiful as thou art bright;
　And welcome is the thought of thee
　　As the fragrance of an eastern night.
　　　　Our hands, &c.

3 Wide earth can give no place of rest,
　　And for sorrow's tale it hath no ear;
　But thou dost echo in thy breast
　　Grief's loud cry, and suffering's silent tear.
　　　　Our hands, &c.

4 We are no longer desolate,
　　Though our sins have stricken us at heart;
　Whom thou didst bear hath borne their weight,
　　And thou wert His partner in the smart.
　　　　Our hands, &c.

5 Calm as the blessed eye of God
　　When it looks o'er all this world below,
　He bids thee shed His peace abroad,
　　With a secret balm for every woe.
　　　　Our hands, &c.

6 By thee we gain, dear spotless Queen,
   Some vision of what our God must be;
And in thy glory His is seen,
   For He shows Himself when He shows thee.
      Our hands, &c.

62.   9.

FOR THE SOULS IN PURGATORY.

1 OH, turn to Jesus, Mother, turn,
   And call Him by His tenderest names;
Pray for the holy souls that burn
   This hour amid the cleansing flames.

2 Ah, they have fought a gallant fight;
   In death's cold arms they persevered;
And after life's uncheery night
   The harbour of their rest is near'd.

3 In pains beyond all earthly pains,
   Favourites of Jesus, there they lie,
Letting the fire wear out their stains,
   And worshiping God's purity.

4 Spouses of Christ they are, for He
   Was wedded to them by His blood;
And angels o'er their destiny
   In wondering adoration brood.

5 They are the children of thy tears;
   Then hasten, Mother, to their aid;
In pity think each hour appears
   An age while glory is delayed.

6 Ah me! the love of Jesus yearns
   O'er that abyss of sacred pain,
And as He looks His bosom burns
   With Calvary's dear thirst again.

7 O Mary, let thy Son no more
   His lingering spouses thus expect;
God's children to their God restore,
   And to the Spirit His elect.

63.

10.

HYMN OF ST. CASIMIR.

1 DAILY, daily, sing to Mary,
   Sing, my soul, her praises due;
All her feasts, her actions worship,
   With the heart's devotion true.
     Lost in wondering contemplation,
      Be her majesty confest;
     Call her Mother, call her Virgin,
      Happy Mother, Virgin blest.

2 She is mighty to deliver;
   Call her, trust her lovingly;
When the tempest rages round thee,
   She will calm the troubled sea.
     Gifts of heaven she has given,
      Noble Lady! to our race;
     She, the Queen, who decks her subjects
      With the light of God's own grace.

3 Sing, my tongue, the Virgin's trophies,
   Who for us her Maker bore;
For the curse of old inflicted,
   Peace and blessing to restore.
     Sing in songs of praise unending,
      Sing the world's majestic Queen;
     Weary not, nor faint in telling
      All the gifts she gives to men.

4 All my senses, heart, affections,
   Strive to sound her glory forth,
Spread abroad the sweet memorials
   Of the Virgin's priceless worth.

Where the voice of music thrilling,
 Where the tongue of eloquence,
That can utter hymns beseeming
 All her matchless excellence?

5 All our joys do flow from Mary;
 All, then, join her praise to sing;
Trembling sing the Virgin Mother,
 Mother of our Lord and King.
  While we sing her awful glory,
   Far above our fancy's reach,
  Let our hearts be quick to offer:
   Love alone the heart can teach.

Part II.

6 Holy Mary, we implore thee
 By thy purity divine;
Help us, bending here before thee,
 Help us truly to be thine.
  Thou, unfolding wide the portals
   Of the kingdom in the skies,
  Holy Virgin, hast to mortals
   Shown the land of paradise.

7 Thou, when deepest night infernal
 Had for ages shrouded man,
Gavest us that light eternal
 Promised since the world began.
  God in thee hath showered plenty
   On the hungry and the weak;
  Sending back the mighty empty,
   Setting up on high the meek.

8 Teach, oh, teach us, holy Mother,
 How to conquer every sin,
How to love and help each other,
 How the prize of life to win.

  Thou to whom a Child was given
   Greater than the sons of men,
  Coming down from highest heaven
   To create this world again.

9 Oh, by that Almighty Maker
  Whom thyself a virgin bore;
Oh, by thy supreme Creator,
  Linked with thee for evermore;
   By the hope thy name inspires;
    By our doom, revers'd through thee,
  Help us, Queen of angel-choirs,
   To a blest eternity.

---

64.   11.

1 MOTHER of our Lord and Saviour,
  First in beauty as in power!
Glory of the Christian nations,
  Ready help in trouble's hour!

2 Though the gates of hell against us
  With profoundest fury rage;
Though the ancient foe assault us,
  And his fiercest battle wage,—

3 Nought can hurt the pure in spirit,
  Who upon thine aid rely;
At thy hand secure of gaining
  Strength and mercy from on high;

4 Safe beneath thy mighty shelter,
  Though a thousand hosts combine.
All must fall or flee before us,
  Scattered by His arm divine.

5 Firm as once on holy Sion
    David's tower rear'd its height,
With a glorious rampart girded,
    And with glistening armour bright;

6 So th' Almighty's Virgin Mother
    Stands in strength for evermore;
From Satanic hosts defending
    All who her defence implore.

7 Through the everlasting ages,
    Blessed Trinity, to Thee,
Father, Son, and Holy Spirit,
    Praise and endless glory be.

---

65.   12.

1 Look down, O Mother Mary,
    From thy bright throne above;
Cast down upon thy children
    One only glance of love.

2 And if a heart so tender
    With pity flows not o'er,
Then turn away, O Mother,
    And look on us no more.

3 O Mary, dearest Mother,
    If thou wouldst have us live,
Say that we are thy children,
    And JESUS will forgive.

4 Our sins make us unworthy
    That title still to bear;
But thou art still our Mother,—
    Then show a mother's care.

5 Open to us thy mantle,
    There stay we without fear;
What evil can befall us,
    If, Mother, thou art near?

6 Oh, sweetest, dearest Mother,
    Thy sinful children save!
Look down on us with pity,
    Who thy protection crave.

13.

Hail, Queen of Heaven, the Ocean Star,
  Guide of the wanderer here below!
Thrown on life's surge, we claim Thy care,
  Save us from peril and from woe.
    Mother of Christ, Star of the Sea,
    Pray for the wanderer, pray for me.

O gentle, chaste, and spotless Maid,
  We sinners make our prayers through thee,
Remind thy Son that He has paid
  The price of our iniquity.
    Virgin most pure, Star of the sea,
    Pray for the sinner, pray for me.

Sojourners in this vale of tears,
  To thee, blest Advocate, we cry,
Pity our sorrows, calm our fears,
  And soothe with hope our misery.
    Refuge in grief, Star of the sea,
    Pray for the mourner, pray for me.

And while to Him who reigns above,
  In Godhead One, in Persons Three,
The Source of life, of grace, of love,
  Homage we pay on bended knee;
    Do thou, bright Queen, Star of the sea,
    Pray for thy children, pray for me.

67.

14.

1 HAIL, bright Star of ocean,
   God's own Mother blest;
Ever-sinless Virgin,
   Gate of heavenly rest!

2 Taking that sweet Ave
   Which from Gabriel came,
Peace confirm within us,
   Changing Eva's name.

3 Break the captive's fetters;
   Light on blindness pour;
All our ills expelling,
   Every bliss implore.

4 Show thyself a mother;
   May the Word divine,
Born for us thine Infant,
   Hear our prayers through thine.

5 Virgin all excelling,
   Mildest of the mild,
Freed from guilt, preserve us
   Meek and undefiled.

6 Keep our life all spotless,
   Make our way secure,
Till we find in Jesus
   Joy for evermore.

7 Through the highest Heaven,
   To the Almighty Three,
Father, Son, and Spirit,
   One same glory be.

68. St. Anne, Mother of our Blessed Mary.

1 SPOTLESS Anna! Juda's glory!
  Through the Church from East to West,
Every tongue proclaims thy praises,
  Holy Mary's Mother blest!

2 Saintly Kings and priestly Sires
  Blended in thy sacred line;
Thou in virtue, all before thee
  Didst excel by grace divine.

3 Link'd in bonds of purest wedlock,
  Thine it was for us to bear,
By the favour of High Heaven,
  Our eternal Virgin Star.

4 From thy stem in beauty budded
  Ancient Jesse's mystic rod:
Earth from thee receiv'd the Mother
  Of th' Almighty Son of God.

5 All the human race benighted
  In the depths of darkness lay;
When in Anne it saw the dawning
  Of the long-expected day.

---

69. The Nativity of the Blessed Virgin Mary.

1 SWEET Morn! thou Parent of the Sun!
  And Daughter of the same!
What joy and gladness, through thy birth,
  This day to mortals came!

2 Clothed in the sun I see thee stand,
    The moon beneath thy feet;
The stars above thy sacred head
    A radiant coronet.

3 Thrones and dominions gird thee round,
    The armies of the sky;
Pure streams of glory from thee flow,
    All bath'd in Deity!

4 Terrific as the banner'd line
    Of battle's dread array!
Before thee tremble Hell and Death,
    And own thy mighty sway:

5 While crushed beneath thy dauntless foot,
    The Serpent writhes in vain;
Smit by a deadly stroke, and bound
    In an eternal chain.

6 O Mightiest! pray for us, that He
    Who came through thee of yore,
May come to dwell within our hearts,
    And never quit us more.

7 Praise to the Father, with the Son,
    And Holy Ghost, through Whom
The Word eternal was conceiv'd
    Within the Virgin's womb.

---

70. The Annunciation of the Blessed Virgin Mary.

1 The Angel spake the word,—
    "Hail, thou of women blest!"
From highest Heav'n the Godhead comes,
    And fills her virgin breast.

2 Maiden! how great henceforth
      Thy dignity shall be!
  The Son of God becomes thine own,
      This day conceived by thee.

3 This day the Holy Ghost
      From thy all-sinless blood
  Moulds in thy womb that Flesh divine
      Of the life-giving Word;

4 Whereby we babes the meat
      Of elder ones obtain;
  And He, who Angels feeds as God,
      Feeds men as God made Man.

5 To Him who, to redeem
      Our race, came down from Heaven,
  Praise with the Father evermore,
      And Holy Ghost, be given.

---

71. 2.

1 WHAT mortal tongue can sing thy praise,
      Dear Mother of the Lord!
  To Angels only it belongs
      Thy glory to record.

2 Who born of man can penetrate
      Thy soul's majestic shrine?
  Who can thy mighty gifts unfold,
      Or rightly them divine?

3 Say, Virgin, what sweet force was that
      Which from the Father's breast
  Drew forth His co-eternal Son,
      To be thy bosom's guest?

4 'Twas not thy guileless faith alone
    That lifted thee so high;
'Twas not thy pure seraphic love,
    Or peerless chastity:

5 But, oh, it was thy lowliness,
    Well pleasing to the Lord,
That made thee worthy to become
    The Mother of the Word.

6 O Loftiest!—whose humility
    So sweet it was to see!
That God, forgetful of Himself,
    Abas'd Himself to thee!

7 Praise to the Father, with the Son,
    And Holy Ghost, through Whom
The Word eternal was conceiv'd
    Within the Virgin's womb.

72. The Visitation of the Blessed Virgin Mary.

1 WHITHER thus, in holy rapture,
    Princely Maiden, art thou bent?
Why so fleetly art thou speeding
    Up the mountain's rough ascent?

2 Fill'd with the Eternal Godhead
    Glowing with the Spirit's flame!
Love it is that bears thee onward,
    And supports thy tender frame.

3 Lo! thine aged cousin claims thee,
    Claims thy sympathy and care;
God her shame from her hath taken;
    He hath heard her fervent prayer.

4 Blessed mothers! joyful meeting!
    Thou in her, the hand of God,
She in thee, with lips inspir'd,
    Owns the Mother of her Lord.

5 As the sun his face concealing,
    In a cloud withdraws from sight,
So in Mary then lay hidden
    He who is the world's true light.

6 Honour, glory, virtue, merit,
    Be to Thee, O Virgin's Son!
With the Father and the Spirit,
    While eternal ages run.

---

73. The Purification of the Blessed Virgin Mary.

1 O Sion! open wide thy gates;
    Let figures disappear;
A Priest and Victim both in one,
    The Truth Himself, is here.

2 No more the simple flock shall bleed.
    Behold the Father's Son,
Himself to His own Altar comes
    For sinners to atone.

3 Conscious of hidden Deity,
    The lowly Virgin brings
Her new-born Babe, with two young doves,
    Her tender offerings.

4 The hoary Simeon sees at last
    His Lord so long desired,
And hails, with Anna, Israel's hope,
    With sudden rapture fired.

5 But silent knelt the Mother blest
    Of the yet silent Word;
And pondering all things in her heart,
    With speechless praise ador'd.

6 Praise to the Father and the Son;
    Praise to the Spirit be;
Praise to the blessed Three in One,
    Through all eternity.

74. The Maternity of the Blessed Virgin Mary.

1 THE Saviour left high Heav'n to dwell
    Within the Virgin's womb;
And there array'd Himself in flesh,
    Our Victim to become.

2 She unto us divinely bore
    Salvation's King and God;
Who died for us upon the Cross,
    Who saves us in His blood.

3 She too our joyful hope shall be,
    And drive away all fears;
Offering for us to her dear Son
    Our contrite sighs and tears.

4 That Son—He hears His Mother's prayer,
    And grants, ere it be said;
Be ours to love her, and invoke
    In every strait her aid.

5 All glory to the Trinity,
    While endless times proceed;
Who in that bosom pure of stain
    Sow'd such immortal seed.

75. The Purity of the Blessed Virgin Mary.

1 Blest Guardian of all virgin souls!
    Portal of bliss to man forgiven!
Pure Mother of Almighty God!
    Thou hope of earth, and joy of Heaven!

2 Fair Lily, found amid the thorns!
    Most beauteous Dove with wings of gold!
Rod from whose tender root there sprang
    That healing Flow'r long since foretold!

3 Thou Tow'r, against the dragon proof!
    Thou Star, to storm-toss'd voyagers dear!
Our course lies o'er a treacherous deep;
    Thine be the light by which we steer.

4 Scatter the mists that round us hang;
    Keep far the fatal shoals away;
And while through darkling waves we sweep,
    Open a path to life and day.

5 O Jesu, born of Virgin bright,
    Immortal glory be to Thee;
Praise to the Father infinite,
    And Holy Ghost eternally.

---

76. Children's Hymn before our Lady's Image in the Month of May.

FIRST CHILD.

This is the image of the Queen
    Who reigns in bliss above;
Of her who is the hope of men,
    Whom men and angels love!

Most holy Mary! at thy feet
  I bend a suppliant knee;
CHORUS. In this thy own sweet Month of May,
  Dear Mother of my God, I pray,
  Do thou remember me!

SECOND CHILD.

The sacred homage that we pay
  To Mary's image here,
To Mary's self at once ascends,
  Above the starry sphere.

Most holy Mary! at thy feet
  I bend a suppliant knee;
CHORUS. In all my joy, in all my pain,
  O Virgin born without a stain,
  Do thou remember me!

THIRD CHILD.

How fair soever be the form
  Which here your eyes behold,
Its beauty is by Mary's self
  Excell'd a thousandfold.

Most holy Mary! at thy feet
  I bend a suppliant knee;
CHORUS. In my temptations, each and all
  The sad effect of Eva's fall,
  Do thou remember me!

FOURTH CHILD.

Sweet are the flow'rets we have cull'd,
  This image to adorn;
But sweeter far is Mary's self,
  That rose without a thorn!

Most holy Mary! at thy feet
  I bend a suppliant knee;
CHORUS. When on the bed of death I lie,
  By Him who did for sinners die,
  Do thou remember me!

FIFTH CHILD.

O Lady, by the stars that make
A glory round thy head ;

SIXTH CHILD.

And by thy pure uplifted hands,
That for thy children plead ;

SEVENTH CHILD.

O Lady, by that face divine
Which angels joy to see ;

EIGHTH CHILD.

And by the deadly serpent's might,
Subdu'd and crushed by thee ;

NINTH CHILD.

And by thy robe of mystic hue,
More azure than the skies ;

TENTH CHILD.

And by those lips suffus'd with grace ;
And by those pitying eyes ;

ELEVENTH CHILD.

And by these freshly gather'd flowers
Here offer'd at thy feet;

TWELFTH CHILD.

And by thy prayers that evermore
Ascend as incense sweet ;—

When at the Judgment-seat I stand,
And my dread Saviour see ;
ALL. When waves of night around me roll,
And Hell is raging for my soul ;
Oh, then remember me !

77. Jesus and Mary.
[For Children.]

1 Jesus and Mary! sounds the sweetest
   That ever fell on mortal ear;
Jesus and Mary! words the meetest
   For earth's poor children to speak or hear;
Jesus and Mary! naught shall sever
   Those sweet Names from our lips and heart:
Jesus and Mary! who shall ever
   Dare to think of the two apart?

2 Jesus and Mary! softly thrilling,
   Breathe those Names in the infant's ear;
Hush! and hark to the angels filling
   Heaven's wide halls with the chorus clear.
Jesus and Mary! naught shall sever, &c.

3 Jesus and Mary! gently utter
   Those dear Names when a danger's near;
Each little heart will cease to flutter;
   Nothing can hurt you, for they are near.
Jesus and Mary! naught shall sever, &c.

4 Jesus and Mary! faintly breathing
   From lips of the dying the sounds we hear;
See how the pale lips are gently wreathing
   A last fond smile for the Name so dear.
Jesus and Mary! naught shall sever, &c.

5 Jesus and Mary! loving-hearted
   Son and Mother most sweet and dear!
Jesus and Mary! never parted,
   Listen and smile on your children here.
Jesus and Mary! naught shall sever, &c.

SEASONS OF THE CHURCH.

78. Advent.

1 O Thou, who Thine own Father's breast
    Forsaking, Word sublime !
Didst come to aid a world distress'd
    In Thy appointed time :

2 Our hearts enlighten with Thy ray,
    And kindle with Thy love;
That, dead to earthly things, we may
    Live but to things above.

3 So when before the Judgment-seat
    The sinner hears his doom,
And when a voice divinely sweet
    Shall call the righteous home ;

4 Safe from the black and fiery flood
    That sweeps the dread abyss,
May we behold the face of God
    In everlasting bliss.

5 Now to the Father, with the Son,
    And Spirit evermore,
Be glory while the ages run,
    As in all time before.

79. 2.

1 Hark ! an awful voice is sounding ;
    "Christ is nigh !" it seems to say ;
"Cast away the dreams of darkness,
    O ye children of the day !"

2 Startled at the solemn warning,
    Let the earth-bound soul arise ;
Christ her Sun, all sloth dispelling,
    Shines upon the morning skies.

3 Lo! the Lamb so long expected
    Comes with pardon down from Heav'n ;
Let us haste with tears of sorrow,
    One and all to be forgiven.

4 So, when next He comes with glory,
    Wrapping all the earth in fear,
May He then as our Defender
    On the clouds of Heav'n appear.

80.   3.

1 CREATOR of the starry frame,
    Eternal light of all who live!
Jesu, Redeemer of mankind!
    An ear to Thy poor suppliants give.

2 When man, o'erwhelm'd in sin and death,
    Was wholly lost in Satan's snare,
Love brought Thee down to cure our ills,
    By taking of those ills a share.

3 Thy love for guilty men it was
    That caused Thy sacred blood to flow ;
When, issuing from Thy virgin shrine,
    Thou didst to death a victim go.

4 Great Judge of all, in that last day,
    When friends shall fail and foes combine,
Look down in pity then, we pray,
    And guard us with Thine arm divine.

5 To God the Father and the Son
    All praise and power and glory be,
With Thee, O sacred Paraclete,
    Both now and through eternity.

---

81.   Christmas.

1 Jesu, Redeemer of the world!
    Who, ere the earliest dawn of light,
Wast from eternal ages born,
    Immense in glory as in might;

2 Immortal Hope of all mankind!
    In whom the Father's face we see;
Hear Thou the prayers Thy people pour
    This day throughout the world to Thee.

3 Remember, O Creator Lord!
    That in the Virgin's sacred womb
Thou wast conceiv'd, and of her flesh
    Didst our mortality assume.

4 This ever-blest returning day
    Its witness bears, that all alone,
From Thy own Father's bosom forth
    To save the world Thou camest down.

5 O Day! to which the seas and sky,
    And earth and Heav'n, glad welcome sing;
O Day! which heal'd our misery,
    And brought on earth salvation's King.

6 We too, O Lord, who have been cleans'd
    In Thy own fount of blood divine,
Offer the tribute of sweet song
    On this blest natal day of Thine.

7 O Jesu! born of Virgin bright,
   Immortal glory be to Thee;
Praise to the Father infinite,
   And Holy Ghost eternally.

82.   2.

(Adeste Fideles.)

1   Ye faithful, approach ye,
    Joyfully triumphing;
Oh, come ye, oh, come ye, to Bethlehem;
    Come and behold ye
    Born the King of angels:
    Oh, come, let us worship,
    Oh, come, let us worship,
Oh, come, let us worship Christ the Lord.

2   God of God,
    Light of Light,
Lo, He disdains not the Virgin's womb:
    Very God,
    Begotten, not created:
Oh, come, let us worship, &c.

3   Sing, quires angelic,
    Io sing exulting;
Sing, all ye citizens of Heaven above,
    Glory to God
    In the highest!
Oh, come, let us worship, &c.

4   Yea, Lord, we greet Thee,
    Born this happy morning;
Jesu, to Thee be glory giv'n;
    Word of the Father
    In our flesh appearing:
Oh, come, let us worship, &c.

83.   3.

1 SEE, amid the winter's snow,
  Born for us on earth below,
  See, the tender Lamb appears,
  Promis'd from eternal years !
    Hail, thou ever-blessed morn !
    Hail, Redemption's happy dawn !
    Sing through all Jerusalem,
    Christ is born in Bethlehem.

2 Lo, within a manger lies
  He who built the starry skies;
  He, who thron'd in height sublime,
  Sits amid the Cherubim !
    Hail, &c.

3 Say, ye holy Shepherds, say,
  What your joyful news to-day;
  Wherefore have ye left your sheep
  On the lonely mountain steep ?
    Hail, &c.

4 " As we watch'd at dead of night,
  Lo, we saw a wond'rous light;
  Angels singing peace on earth,
  Told us of the Saviour's birth."
    Hail, &c.

5 Sacred Infant all divine,
  What a tender love was Thine,
  Thus to come from highest bliss,
  Down to such a world as this !
    Hail, &c.

6 Teach, O teach us, holy Child,
  By Thy face so meek and mild,
  Teach us to resemble Thee
  In Thy sweet humility !
    Hail, &c.

7 Virgin Mother, Mary blest,
By the joys that fill thy breast,
Pray for us that we may prove
Worthy of our Saviour's love.
    Hail, &c.

84.   Epiphany.

1 O CRUEL Herod! why thus fear
    Thy King and God, who comes below?
No earthly crown comes He to take,
    Who heavenly kingdoms doth bestow.

2 The wiser Magi see the star,
    And follow as it leads before;
By its pure ray they seek the Light,
    And with their gifts that Light adore.

3 Behold at length the heavenly Lamb
    Baptis'd in Jordan's sacred flood;
There consecrating by His torch
    Water to cleanse us in His blood.

4 But Cana saw her glorious Lord
    Begin His miracles divine;
When water, reddening at His word,
    Flow'd forth obedient in wine.

5 To Thee, O Jesu, who Thyself
    Hast to the Gentile world display'd,
Praise, with the Father evermore,
    And with the Holy Ghost, be paid.

85.   2.

1 NONE of all the noblest cities,
    Bethlem, can with thee compare;
Thou alone the Lord from Heaven
    Didst for us incarnate bear.
Fairer than the beam of morning
    Was the star that told His birth,
To the lands their God announcing,
    Hid beneath a form of earth.

2 By its ray divinely guided,
    See the Eastern kings appear;
See them bend their gifts to offer,—
    Gifts of incense, gold, and myrrh.
Sacred types of mystic meaning:
    Incense doth the God disclose,
Gold a royal child proclaimeth,
    Myrrh a future tomb foreshows.

3 Holy Jesu, in Thy brightness
    To the Gentile world reveal'd,
Still to babes Thyself disclosing,
    Ever from the proud conceal'd—
Honour, glory, virtue, merit,
    Be to Thee, O Virgin Son,
With the Father and the Spirit,
    While eternal ages run.

86.   Lent.

1 THOU loving Maker of mankind,
    Before Thy throne we pray and weep;
Oh, strengthen us with grace divine,
    Duly this sacred Lent to keep.

2 Searcher of hearts! Thou dost our ills
    Discern, and all our weakness know:
Again to Thee with tears we turn;
    Again to us Thy mercy show.

3 Much have we sinn'd; but we confess
    Our guilt, and all our faults deplore:
Oh, for the praise of Thy great Name,
    Our fainting souls to health restore!

4 And grant us, while by fasts we strive
    This mortal body to control,
To fast from all the food of sin,
    And so to purify the soul.

5 Hear us, O Trinity thrice blest!
    Sole Unity! to Thee we cry:
Vouchsafe us from these fasts below
    To reap immortal fruit on high.

87.   2.

1 Now with the slow revolving year,
    Again the Fast we greet;
Which in its mystic circle moves
    Of forty days complete.

2 That Fast, by Law and Prophets taught,
    By Jesus Christ restor'd;
Jesus, of seasons and of times
    The Maker and the Lord.

3 Henceforth more sparing let us be
    Of food, of words, of sleep;
Henceforth beneath a stricter guard
    The roving senses keep.

4 And let us shun whatever things
    Distract the careless heart;
And let us shut the soul against
    The tyrant Tempter's art;

5 And weep before the Judge, and strive
    His vengeance to appease;
Saying to Him with contrite voice,
    Upon our bended knees:

6 " Much have we sinn'd, O Lord! and still
    We sin each day we live;
Yet pour Thy pity from on high,
    And of Thy grace forgive.

7 Remember that we still are Thine,
    Though of a fallen frame;
And take not from us in Thy wrath
    The glory of Thy Name.

8 Undo past evil; grant us, Lord,
    More grace to do aright;
So may we now and ever find
    Acceptance in Thy sight."

9 Blest Trinity in Unity!
    Vouchsafe us, in Thy love,
To gather from these fasts below
    Immortal fruit above.

---

88.   3.

1 SING, my tongue, the Saviour's glory;
    Tell His triumph far and wide;
Tell aloud the famous story
    Of His Body crucified;
How upon the Cross a Victim,
    Vanquishing in death, He died.

2 Eating of the Tree forbidden,
   Man had sunk in Satan's snare,
When our pitying Creator
   Did this second Tree prepare;
Destin'd, many ages later,
   That first evil to repair.

3 Such the order God appointed
   When for sin He would atone;
To the Serpent thus opposing
   Schemes yet deeper than his own;
Thence the remedy procuring,
   Whence the fatal wound had come.

4 So when now at length the fullness
   Of the sacred time drew nigh,
Then the Son, the world's Creator,
   Left His Father's throne on high;
From a Virgin's womb appearing,
   Cloth'd in our mortality.

5 All within a lowly manger,
   Lo, a tender babe He lies!
See his gentle Virgin mother
   Lull to sleep His infant cries!
While the limbs of God Incarnate
   Round with swathing bands she ties.

---

89.   4.

1 Thus did Christ to perfect manhood
   In our mortal flesh attain:
Then of His free choice He goeth
   To a death of bitter pain;
And as a lamb, upon the altar
   Of the Cross, for us is slain.

2 Lo, with gall His thirst He quenches!
   See the thorns upon His brow!
Nails His tender flesh are rending!
   See, His side is open'd now!
Whence, to cleanse the whole creation,
   Streams of blood and water flow.

3 Lofty Tree, bend down thy branches
   To embrace thy sacred load;
Oh, relax the native tension
   Of that all too rigid wood;
Gently, gently bear the members
   Of thy dying King and God.

4 Tree, which solely wast found worthy
   The world's great Victim to sustain!
Harbour from the raging tempest!
   Ark, that sav'd the world again!
Tree, with sacred Blood anointed
   Of the Lamb for sinners slain!

5 Blessing, honour everlasting,
   To the immortal Deity;
To the Father, Son, and Spirit,
   Equal praises ever be:
Glory through the earth and Heaven
   To Trinity in Unity.

---

90. Low Sunday, and through Easter to Ascension-Day.

1 Now at the Lamb's high royal feast
   In robes of saintly white we sing,
Through the Red Sea in safety brought
   By Jesus our immortal King.

2 Oh, depth of love! for us He drinks
    The chalice of His agony;
For us a Victim on the Cross
    He meekly lays Him down to die.

3 And as the avenging Angel pass'd
    Of old the blood-besprinkled door;
As the cleft sea a passage gave,
    Then clos'd to whelm th' Egyptians o'er:

4 So Christ, our Paschal Sacrifice,
    Has brought us safe all perils through;
While for unleaven'd bread we need
    But heart sincere and purpose true.

5 Hail, purest Victim Heav'n could find,
    The powers of Hell to overthrow!
Who didst the chains of Death destroy;
    Who dost the prize of Life bestow.

6 Hail, victor Christ! hail, risen King!
    To Thee alone belongs the crown;
Who hast the heavenly gates unbarr'd,
    And dragg'd the Prince of darkness down.

7 O Jesu! from the death of sin
    Keep us, we pray; so shalt Thou be
The everlasting paschal joy
    Of all the souls new-born in Thee.

8 Now to the Father, and the Son
    Who rose from death, be glory given;
With Thee, O holy Comforter,
    Henceforth by all in earth and Heaven.

1.   2.

1 O THOU, the Heaven's eternal King!
   Lord of the starry spheres!
 Who with the Father equal art
   From everlasting years;

2 All praise to Thy most holy Name,
   Who, when the world began,
 Yoking the soul with clay, didst form
   In Thine own image man.

3 And praise to Thee, who, when the Foe
   Had marr'd Thy work sublime,
 Clothing Thyself in flesh, didst mould
   Our race a second time.

4 When from the tomb new born, as from
   A Virgin born before,
 Thou didst reverse our fallen state,
   And life to man restore.

5 Eternal Shepherd! who Thy flock
   In Thy pure Font dost lave,
 Where souls are cleans'd, and all their guilt
   Buried as in a grave;

6 Jesu! who to the Cross wast nail'd,
   Our countless debt to pay;
 Jesu! who lavishly didst pour
   Thy blood for us away:

7 Oh, from the wretched death of sin
   Keep us! so shalt Thou be
 The everlasting Paschal joy
   Of all new born in Thee.

8 To God the Father, and the Son
   Who rose, be glory given;
 With Thee, Almighty Paraclete,
   By all in earth and Heaven.

92. Easter.

1 Christ the Lord is ris'n to-day:
Christians, haste your vows to pay;
Offer ye your praises meet
At the Paschal Victim's feet.
    For the sheep the Lamb hath bled,
    Sinless in the sinner's stead;
    Christ the Lord is ris'n on high,
    Now He lives no more to die.

2 Christ, the Victim undefil'd,
Man to God hath reconcil'd;
Whilst in strange and awful strife
Met together Death and Life.
    Christians, on this happy day
    Haste with joy your vows to pay;
    Christ the Lord is ris'n on high,
    Now He lives no more to die.

3 Say, O wond'ring Mary, say,
What thou sawest on thy way.
"I beheld, where Christ had lain,
Empty tomb and angels twain;
    I beheld the glory bright
    Of the rising Lord of light:
    Christ my hope is ris'n again,
    Now He lives, and lives to reign."

4 Christ, who once for sinners bled,
Now the firstborn from the dead,
Thron'd in endless might and power,
Lives and reigns for evermore.
    Hail, eternal hope on high!
    Hail, thou King of victory!
    Hail, thou Prince of life ador'd!
    Help and save us, gracious Lord!

93.

2.

1 YE sons and daughters of the Lord!
The King of glory, King ador'd,
This day Himself from death restor'd.

2 All in the early morning gray
Went holy women on their way,
To see the tomb where Jesus lay.

3 Of spices pure a precious store
In their pure hands those women bore,
T' anoint the sacred Body o'er.

4 Then straightway one in white they see,
Who said: "Ye seek the Lord; but He
Is risen, and gone to Galilee."

5 This told they Peter, told they John,
Who forthwith to the tomb are gone;
But Peter is by John outrun.

6 That self-same night, while out of fear
The doors were shut, their Lord most dear
To His Apostles did appear.

7 But Thomas, when of this he heard,
Was doubtful of his brethren's word;
Wherefore again there came the Lord:

8 "Thomas, behold My side," saith He;
"My hands, My feet, My body see,
And doubt not, but believe in Me."

9 When Thomas saw that wounded side,
The truth no longer he denied;
"Thou art my Lord and God!" he cried.

10 Oh, blest are they who have not seen
Their Lord, and yet believe in Him!
Eternal life awaiteth them.

11 Now let us praise the Lord most high,
　　And strive His name to magnify
　On this great day through earth and sky:

12 Whose mercy ever runneth o'er;
　　Whom men and Angel Hosts adore ;
　To Him be glory evermore.

94.   Jesus risen.

1 ALL hail, dear Conqueror! all hail !
　　Oh, what a victory is thine !
　How beautiful Thy strength appears,
　　Thy crimson wounds how bright they shine!

2 Thou camest at the dawn of day:
　　Armies of souls around Thee were,
　Blest spirits thronging to adore
　　Thy Flesh, so marvellous, so fair.

3 The everlasting Godhead lay
　　Shrouded within those Limbs Divine,
　Nor left untenanted one hour
　　That Sacred Human Heart of Thine.

4 They worshiped Thee, those ransomed souls,
　　With the fresh strength of love set free ;
　They worshiped joyously, and thought
　　Of Mary while they looked on Thee.

5 And Thou too, Soul of Jesus ! Thou
　　Towards that sacred Flesh didst yearn,
　And for the beatings of that Heart
　　How ardently Thy love did burn !

6 They worshiped, while the beauteous Soul
　　Paused by the Body's wounded Side :—
　Bright flashed the cave—before them stood
　　The Living Jesus glorified.

7 Ye Heavens, how sang they in your courts,
    How sang the angelic choirs that day,
When from His tomb the imprisoned God,
    Like the strong sunrise, broke away!

8 Down, down, all lofty things on earth,
    And worship Him with joyous dread!
O Sin! thou art undone by love!
    O Death! thou art discomfited!

95.   Ascension.

1 O THOU eternal King most high,
    Who didst the world redeem;
And conquering death and hell, receive
    A dignity supremo:

2 Thou to Thy heavenly throne this day
    Didst in Thy might ascend;
Thenceforth to reign in sovereign power,
    And glory without end.

3 There seated in Thy majesty,
    To Thee submissive bow
The spacious earth, the highest heaven,
    The depths of hell below.

4 There, waiting for Thy faithful souls,
    Be Thou to us, O Lord,
Our peerless joy while here we stay,
    In Heav'n our great reward.

5 Renew our strength; our sins forgive;
    Our miseries efface;
And lift our souls aloft to Thee,
    By Thy celestial grace.

6 So, when Thou shinest on the clouds,
  With Thy angelic train,
 May we be sav'd from vengeance due,
  And our lost crowns regain!

96.   2.

1 O Thou, in whom my love doth find
  Its rest and perfect end;
 O Jesu, Saviour of mankind,
  And their eternal friend!

2 Return, return, pure Light of light,
  To Thy dread throne again;
 Go forth victorious from the fight,
  And in Thy glory reign.

3 Ye Heav'ns, your gates eternal raise,
  Come forth to meet your King;
 Come forth with joy, and sing His praise,—
  His praise eternal sing!

4 O fount of mercy! Light of Heaven!
  Our darkness cast away;
 And grant us all, through Thee forgiven,
  To see the perfect day.

5 Christ to His Father is return'd,
  And sits upon His throne;
 For Him my panting heart hath yearn'd,
  And after Him is gone.

6 To Him praise, glory, without end,
  And adoration be;
 O Jesu, grant us to ascend,
  And reign in Heav'n with Thee!

97.
3.

1 O Thou pure light of souls that love,
 True joy of every human breast,
Sower of life's immortal seed,
 Our Maker, and Redeemer blest!

2 What wondrous pity Thee o'ercame
 To make our guilty load Thine own,
And sinless, suffer death and shame,
 For our transgressions to atone!

3 Thou, bursting Hades open wide,
 Didst all the captive souls unchain;
And thence to Thy dread Father's side
 With glorious pomp ascend again.

4 Jesu! may pity Thee compel
 To heal the wounds of which we die
And take us in Thy Light to dwell,
 Who for Thy blissful Presence sigh.

98.   The Ascension.

1 Why is thy face so lit with smiles,
 Mother of Jesus! why?
And wherefore is thy beaming look
 So fixed upon the sky?

2 From out thine overflowing eyes
 Bright lights of gladness part,
As though some gushing fount of joy
 Had broken in thy heart.

3 Mother! how canst thou smile to-day?
 How can thine eyes be bright,
When He, thy Life, thy Love, thine All,
 Hath vanished from thy sight?

4 His rising form on Olivet
   A summer's shadow cast;
 The branches of the hoary trees
   Drooped as the shadow passed.

5 And as He rose with all His train
   Of righteous souls around,
 His blessing fell into thine heart,
   Like dew into the ground.

6 The Feet which thou hast kissed so oft,
   Those living Feet, are gone;
 Mother! thou canst but stoop and kiss
   Their print upon the stone.

7 Yes! He hath left thee, Mother dear,
   His throne is far above;
 How canst thou be so full of joy,
   When thou hast lost thy Love?

8 Oh, surely earth's poor sunshine now
   To thee mere gloom appears,
 When He is gone who was its light
   For three-and-thirty years.

99.   2.

1 Come, Holy Ghost, Thy grace inspire!
 Who from the Son as from the Sire
   Dost equally proceed;
 Within our hearts divinely glow,
 Our lips with eloquence endow,
   And strengthen us in need.

2 Thou to the lowly dost display
 The beautiful and perfect way
   Of justice and of peace;

Avoiding every stubborn heart,
Thou to the simple dost impart
    True wisdom's rich increase.

3 Teach us to aim at Heav'n's high prize,
  And for its glory to despise
    The world and all below:
Cleanse us from sin; direct us right;
Illuminate us with Thy light;
    Thy peace on us bestow:

4 And as Thou didst in days of old
  On the first Shepherds of the Fold
    In tongues of flame descend,
Now also on its Pastors shine,
And flood with fire of grace divine
    The world from end to end!

5 So unto Thee, who with the Son
  And Father art for ever One,
    The Lord of earth and heaven,
Be, through eternal length of days,
All honour, glory, blessing, praise,
    And adoration, given!

---

100.   3.

1   GRACE Increate!
    From whose informing fire
All acts that to immortal glory tend
    Their force acquire!

2   Hail, Life of life!
    Hail, Paraclete divine!
All justice, sanctity, obedience, love,
    And truth, are thine.

3 Thou in the blood
Of Him who died for men,
By sacramental element applied,
Dost wash us clean.

4 Thou to the deeds
Of every passing hour
In Thee perform'd, impartest merit new
And heavenly power.

5 From grace to grace,
Oh, grant me to proceed;
And with assisting hand my faltering steps
To Sion lead.

6 So may I mount
In peace the holy hill;
And safe at last by life's eternal fount,
There drink my fill.

101. The Descent of the Holy Ghost.

1 O MIGHTY Mother! why that light
In thine uplifted eye?
Why that resplendent look of more
Than queen-like majesty?

2 Oh, waitest thou in this thy joy
For Gabriel once again?
Is heaven about to part, and make
The Blessed Vision plain?

3 She sat; beneath her shadow were
The Chosen of her Son;
Within each heart and on each face
Her power and spirit shone.

4 Queen of the Church! around thee shines
   The purest light of heaven,
And all created things to thee
   For thy domain are given!

5 Why waitest thou then, so abashed,
   Wrapt in ecstatic fear,
Speechless with adoration, hushed,—
   Hushed as though God were near?

6 She is a creature! See! she bows,
   She trembles though so great;—
Created Majesty o'erwhelmed
   Before the Increate!

7 He comes! He comes! That mighty Breath
   From heaven's eternal shores;
His uncreated freshness fills
   His Bride as she adores.

8 Earth quakes before that rushing blast,
   Heaven echoes back the sound,
And mightily the tempest wheels
   That upper room around.

9 One moment—and the Spirit hung
   O'er her with dread desire;
Then broke upon the heads of all
   In cloven tongues of fire.

10 Who knows in what a sea of love
   Our Lady's heart He drowned?
Or what new gifts He gave her then?
   What ancient gifts He crowned?

11 Grace was so multiplied on her,
   So grew within her heart,
She stands alone, earth's miracle,
   A being all apart.

12 What gifts He gave those chosen men,
    Past ages can display;
  Nay, more, their vigour still inspires
    The weakness of to-day.

13 Oh, let us fall and worship Him,
    The Love of Sire and Son,
  The Consubstantial Breath of God,
    The Coeternal One!

---

102.   Corpus Christi.

1 JESUS! my Lord, my God, my all!
    How can I love Thee as I ought?
  And how revere this wondrous gift,
    So far surpassing hope or thought?
      Sweet Sacrament! we Thee adore!
      Oh, make us love Thee more and more!

2 Had I but Mary's sinless heart
    To love Thee with, my dearest King!
  Oh, with what bursts of fervent praise
    Thy goodness, Jesus, would I sing!
      Sweet Sacrament! we Thee adore!
      Oh, make us love Thee more and more!

3 Oh, see! within a creature's hand
    The vast Creator deigns to be,
  Reposing infant-like, as though
    On Joseph's arm, or Mary's knee.
      Sweet Sacrament! we Thee adore!
      Oh, make us love Thee more and more!

4 Thy Body, Soul, and Godhead, all!
    O mystery of love divine!
  I cannot compass all I have,
    For all Thou hast and art are mine!
      Sweet Sacrament! we Thee adore!
      Oh, make us love Thee more and more!

5 Sound, sound His praises higher still,
   And come, ye angels, to our aid,
'Tis God! 'tis God! the very God,
   Whose power both man and angels made!
   Sweet Sacrament! we Thee adore!
   Oh, make us love Thee more and more!

103. Sequence, Whit-Sunday.

1 HOLY Spirit! Lord of light!
   From Thy clear celestial height,
     Thy pure beaming radiance give:

2 Come, Thou Father of the poor!
   Come, with treasures which endure!
     Come, Thou Light of all that live!

3 Thou, of all consolers best,
   Visiting the troubled breast,
     Dost refreshing peace bestow;

4 Thou in toil art comfort sweet;
   Pleasant coolness in the heat;
     Solace in the midst of woe.

5 Light immortal! light divine!
   Visit Thou these hearts of Thine,
     And our inmost being fill.

6 If Thou take Thy grace away,
   Nothing pure in man will stay;
     All his good is turn'd to ill.

7 Heal our wounds—our strength renew;
   On our dryness pour Thy dew;
     Wash the stains of guilt away:

8 Bend the stubborn heart and will;
   Melt the frozen, warm the chill:
      Guide the steps that go astray.

9 Thou, on those who evermore
   Thee confess and Thee adore,
      In Thy sevenfold gifts descend:

10 Give them comfort when they die;
   Give them life with Thee on high;
      Give them joys which never end.

104. Sequence, Solemnity of Corpus Christi.

1 Sion, lift thy voice, and sing;
   Praise thy Saviour and thy King;
      Praise with hymns thy Shepherd true:
   Strive thy best to praise Him well:
   Yet doth He all praise excel;
      None can ever reach His due.

2 See to-day before us laid
   The living and life-giving Bread!
      Theme for praise and joy profound!
   The same which at the sacred board
   Was, by our Incarnate Lord,
      Giv'n to His Apostles round.

3 Let the praise be loud and high:
   Sweet and tranquil be the joy
      Felt to-day in every breast;
   On this Festival divine,
   Which records the origin
      Of the glorious Eucharist.

4 On this Table of the King,
  Our new Paschal offering
    Brings to end the olden rite;
  Here, for empty shadows fled,
  Is Reality instead ;
    Here, instead of darkness, Light.

5 His own act, at supper seated,
  Christ ordain'd to be repeated,
    In His Memory divine;
  Wherefore now, with adoration,
  We the Host of our salvation
    Consecrate from bread and wine.

6 Hear what holy Church maintaineth,
  That the bread its substance changeth
    Into Flesh, the wine to Blood.
  Doth it pass thy comprehending?
  Faith, the law of sight transcending,
    Leaps to things not understood.

7 Here, beneath these signs, are hidden
  Priceless things, to sense forbidden ;
    Signs, not things, are all we see ;—
  Flesh from bread, and Blood from wine;
  Yet is Christ, in either sign,
    All entire, confess'd to be.

8 They too, who of Him partake,
  Sever not, nor rend, nor break,
    But entire, their Lord receive.
  Whether one or thousands eat,
  All receive the self-same meat,
    Nor the less for others leave.

9 Both the wicked and the good
  Eat of this celestial Food;
    But with ends how opposite!
  Here 'tis life, and there 'tis death ;
  The same, yet issuing to each
    In a difference infinite.

10 Nor a single doubt retain,
　　When they break the Host in twain,
　　But that in each part remains
　　　　What was in the whole before;
　　Since the simple sign alone
　　Suffers change in state or form,
　　The Signified remaining One
　　　　And the Same for evermore.

11 Lo! upon the Altar lies,
　　Hidden deep from human eyes,
　　Bread of Angels from the skies,
　　　　Made the food of mortal man:
　　Children's meat to dogs denied;
　　In old types foresignified;
　　In the manna Heav'n-supplied,
　　　　Isaac, and the Paschal Lamb.

12 Jesu! Shepherd of the sheep!
　　Thou Thy flock in safety keep.
　　Living Bread! Thy life supply;
　　Strengthen us, or else we die;
　　　　Fill us with celestial grace:
　　Thou, who feedest us below!
　　Source of all we have or know!
　　Grant that with Thy Saints above,
　　Sitting at the feast of love,
　　　　We may see Thee face to face.

---

105. Feast of Corpus Christi.

1 SING, my tongue, the Saviour's glory,
　　Of His Flesh the mystery sing;
　Of the Blood, all price exceeding,
　　Shed by our immortal King,
　Destin'd, for the world's redemption,
　　From a noble womb to spring.

2 Of a pure and spotless Virgin
    Born for us on earth below,
He, as Man with man conversing,
    Stay'd, the seeds of truth to sow;
Then He clos'd in solemn order
    Wondrously His life of woe.

3 On the night of that Last Supper,
    Seated with His chosen band,
He the paschal victim eating,
    First fulfils the Law's command;
Then, as Food to all His brethren
    Gives Himself with His own hand.

4 Word made Flesh, the bread of nature
    By his word to Flesh He turns;
Wine into His Blood He changes:—
    What though sense no change discerns?
Only be the heart in earnest,
    Faith her lesson quickly learns.

5 Down in adoration falling,
    Lo! the sacred Host we hail;
Lo! o'er ancient forms departing,
    Newer rites of grace prevail;
Faith, for all defects supplying,
    Where the feeble senses fail.

6 To the Everlasting Father,
    And the Son who reigns on high,
With the Holy Ghost proceeding
    Forth from Each eternally,
Be salvation, honour, blessing,
    Might, and endless majesty.

106. St. Michael.

1 Hail, bright Archangel! Prince of heaven!
   Spirit divinely strong!
To whose rare merit hath been given
   To head the angelic throng!

2 Thine the first worship was, when gloom
   Through heaven's thinned ranks did move,
Thus giving unto God the bloom
   Of young creation's love.

3 First servant of the Ineffable!
   The first created eye
That ever, proved and perfect, fell
   On the dread Trinity!

4 O Michael! worship Him this night,
   The Father, Word, and Dove,
Renewing with strong act the might
   Of thy first marvellous love.

5 Praise to the Three, whose love designed
   Thee champion of the Lord;
Who first conceived thee in His mind,
   And made thee with His Word.

6 Who stooped from nothingness to raise
   A life like thine so high,
Beauty and being that should praise
   His love eternally!

107. St. Gabriel.

1 Hail, Gabriel! hail! a thousand hails
   For thine whose music still prevails
     In the world's listening ear!
Angelic Word! sent forth to tell
How the Eternal Word should dwell
     Amid His creatures here!

2 Angel of Jesus! days gone by
   Bore burdens of kind prophecy
      To quicken hope delayed;
   Then, preluding with John's sweet name,
   At length thy choicest music came
      Unto the Mother-Maid.

3 Voice of heaven's sweetness, uttered low,
   Thy words like strains of music grow
      Upon the stilly night:
   Clear echoes from the Mind of God,
   Stealing through Mary's blest abode
      In pulses of delight.

4 O Voice! dear Voice! the ages hear
   That Hail of thine still lingering near,
      An unexhausted song:
   And still thou com'st with balmy wing,
   And oh! thou seemest still to sing,
      Thine Ave to prolong.

5 O blessed Gabriel! Tongue of God!
   Sweet-spoken Spirit! thou hast showed
      To us the Word-made Man;
   He bade thee break His silence here;
   The tale thou told'st in Mary's ear
      His coming scarce foreran.

6 Joseph and John were, like to thee,
   Chosen for Mary's custody,
      In her retired abode.
   O Gabriel! get us love like theirs,
   For her whose unremitting prayers
      Have gained us love of God!

7 Take up in Heaven for us thy part,
   And, singing to the Sacred Heart,
      Thy strains of rapture raise;
   And tune with endless Ave still
   The voices of the Blessed, and fill
      The Ear of God with praise!

108. St. Raphael the Archangel.

1 Jesu, brightness of the Father!
    Life and strength of all who live!
In the presence of the Angels,
    Glory to Thy name we give;
And Thy wondrous praise rehearse,
Singing in alternate verse.

2 Hail, too, ye angelic powers!
    Hail, ye thrones celestial!
Hail, Physician of Salvation!
    Guide of life, blest Raphael!
Who the Foe of all mankind
Didst in links of iron bind.

3 Oh, may Christ, by thy protection,
    Shelter us from harm this day;
Keep us pure in flesh and spirit;
    Save us from the enemy;
And vouchsafe us, of His grace,
In His Paradise a place.

4 Glory to th' Almighty Father,
    Sing we now in anthems sweet;
Glory to the great Redeemer;
    Glory to the Paraclete;
Three in One, and One in Three,
Throughout all eternity.

---

109. The Guardian Angel.

1 Dear Angel! ever at my side,
    How loving must thou be,
To leave thy home in Heaven to guard
    A guilty wretch like me!

2 Thy beautiful and shining face
   I see not, though so near;
 The sweetness of thy soft low voice
   I am too deaf to hear.

3 I cannot feel thee touch my hand
   With pressure light and mild,
 To check me, as my mother did
   When I was but a child.

4 But I have felt thee in my thoughts
   Fighting with sin for me;
 And when my heart loves God, I know
   The sweetness is from thee.

5 And when, dear Spirit! I kneel down,
   Morning and night, to prayer,
 Something there is within my heart
   Which tells me thou art there.

6 Yes! when I pray thou prayest too—
   Thy prayer is all for me;
 But when I sleep, thou sleepest not,
   But watchest patiently.

7 But most of all I feel thee near,
   When, from the good priest's feet,
 I go absolved, in fearless love,
   Fresh toils and cares to meet.

8 And thou in life's last hour wilt bring
   A fresh supply of grace,
 And afterwards wilt let me kiss
   Thy beautiful bright face.

9 Ah me! how lovely they must be
   Whom God has glorified!
 Yet one of them, oh, sweetest thought!
   Is ever at my side.

10 Then, for thy sake, dear Angel! now
    More humble will I be:
But I am weak; and when I fall,
    Oh, weary not of me:

11 Oh, weary not, but love me still,
    For Mary's sake, thy Queen;
She never tired of me, though I
    Her worst of sons have been.

12 She will reward thee with a smile;
    Thou know'st what it is worth!
For Mary's smiles each day convert
    The hardest hearts on earth.

13 Then love me, love me, Angel dear!
    And I will love thee more;
And help me when my soul is cast
    Upon the eternal shore.

---

110.   St. Peter.

1 Peter, blest Shepherd! hear our piteous cry,
    And with a word unloose our guilty chain;
Thou! who hast pow'r to ope the gates on high
To mortal man, and pow'r to shut them fast again.

2 Praise, blessing, majesty, through endless days,
    Be to the Trinity immortal given;
Who in pure Unity profoundly sways
Eternally alike all things in earth and Heaven.

111. St. Paul.

1 LEAD us, great teacher Paul, in wisdom's ways,
    And lift our hearts with thine to Heaven's high throne ;
Till Faith beholds the clear meridian blaze,
And sunlike in the soul reigns Charity alone.

2 Praise, blessing, majesty, through endless days,
    Be to the Trinity immortal given ;
Who in pure Unity profoundly sways
Eternally all things alike in earth and Heaven.

112. St. Peter and St. Paul.

1 IT is no earthly summer's ray
    That sheds this golden brightness round,
Crowning with heavenly light the day
    The Princes of the Church were crowned.

2 The blessed Seer, to whom were given
    The hearts of men to teach and school ;
And he that keeps the keys of heaven,
    For those on earth that own his rule ;—

3 Fathers of mighty Rome ! whose word
    Shall pass the doom of life or death,
By humble cross and bleeding sword
    Well have they won their laurel-wreath.

4 O happy Rome ! made holy now
    By these two martyrs' glorious blood ;
Earth's best and fairest cities bow,
    By thy superior claims subdued.

5 . For thou alone art worth them all,
   City of martyrs! thou alone
Canst cheer our pilgrim hearts, and call
   The Saviour's sheep to Peter's throne.

6 All honour, power, and praise be given
   To Him who reigns in bliss on high,
For endless, endless years in heaven,
   One only God in Trinity!
                     Amen.

113. St. John the Evangelist.

1 SAINT of the Sacred Heart,
  Sweet teacher of the Word,
  Partner of Mary's woes,
  And favourite of thy Lord!

2 Thou to whom grace was given
  To stand when Peter fell;
  Whose heart could brook the Cross
  Of Him it loved so well!

3 We know not all thy gifts;
  But this Christ bids us see,
  That He who so loved all
  Found more to love in thee.

4 When the last evening came,
  Thy head was on His breast,
  Pillowed on earth, where now
  In Heaven the saints find rest.

5 God and His friend, so free
  To touch, to rest, to move,
  The angels wondering gazed,
  And envied human love.

6 Dear Saint! I stand far off,
  With vilest sins opprest;
  O may I dare, like thee,
  To lean upon His breast?

7 His touch could heal the sick,
  His voice could raise the dead;
  Oh, that my soul might be
  Where He allows thy head!

8 The gifts He gave to thee
  He gave thee to impart;
  And I, too, claim with thee
  His Mother and His Heart!

114.   2.

1 THE life which God's Incarnate Word
    Liv'd here below with men,
  Three blest Evangelists record,
    With Heav'n-inspired pen:

2 John penetrates on eagle wing
    The Father's dread abode;
  And shows the mystery wherein
    The Word subsists with God.

3 Pure Saint! upon his Saviour's breast
    Invited to recline,
  'Twas thence he drew, in moments blest,
    His knowledge all divine:

4 There, too, with that angelic love
    Did he his bosom fill,
  Which, once enkindled from above,
    Breathes in his pages still.

5 Oh, dear to Christ!—to thee upon
  His Cross, of all bereft,
Thou Virgin soul! the Virgin Son
  His Virgin Mother left.

115. 3.

1 An exile for the Faith
  Of thy Incarnate Lord,
Beyond the stars,—beyond all space,
  Thy soul unprison'd soar'd:

2 There saw in glory Him
  Who liveth, and was dead;
There Judah's Lion, and the Lamb
  That for our ransom bled:

3 There of the Kingdom learnt
  The mysteries sublime,—
How, sown in Martyrs' blood, the Faith
  Should spread from clime to clime.

4 There the new City, bath'd
  In her dear Spouse's light,
Pure seat of bliss, thy spirit saw,
  And gloried in the sight.

5 Now to the Lamb's clear fount,
  To drink of life their fill,
Thou callest all;—O Lord, in me
  This blessed thirst instil.

6 To Jesus, Virgin-born,
  Praise with the Father be;
Praise to the Spirit Paraclete,
  Through all eternity.

116. St. Joseph.

1 Hail! holy Joseph, hail!
Husband of Mary, hail!
Chaste as the lily flower
In Eden's peaceful vale.

2 Hail! holy Joseph, hail!
Father of Christ esteemed!
Father be thou to those
Thy Foster-Son redeemed.

3 Hail! holy Joseph, hail!
Prince of the house of God;
May His best graces be
By thy sweet hands bestowed.

4 Hail! holy Joseph, hail!
Comrade of angels, hail!
Cheer thou the hearts that faint,
And guide the steps that fail.

5 Hail! holy Joseph, hail!
God's choice wert thou alone;
To thee the Word made flesh
Was subject as a Son.

6 Hail! holy Joseph, hail!
Teach us our flesh to tame;
And, Mary, keep the hearts
That love thy husband's name.

7 Mother of Jesus! bless,
And bless, ye Saints on high,
All meek and simple souls
That to St. Joseph cry.

117. St. Mary Magdalene.

1 FATHER of lights! one glance of Thine,
　　Whose eyes the Universe control,
Fills Magdalene with holy love,
　　And melts the ice within her soul.

2 Her precious ointment forth she brings
　　Upon those sacred feet to pour;
She washes them with burning tears;
　　And with her hair she wipes them o'er.

3 Impassion'd to the Cross she clings;
　　Nor fears beside the tomb to stay;
Of ruffian soldiers nought she recks,
　　For love has cast all fear away.

4 O Christ, Thou very Love itself!
　　Blest hope of man, through Thee forgiven!
So touch our spirits from above,
　　And purify our souls for Heaven.

118.　　　　2.

1 SON of the Highest! deign to cast
　　On us a pitying eye;
Thou, who repentant Magdalene
　　Didst call to endless joy.

2 Again the royal treasury
　　Receives its long-lost coin;
The gem is found, and, cleans'd from mire,
　　Doth all the stars outshine.

3 O Jesu! balm of every wound!
　　The sinner's only stay!
Wash Thou in Magdalene's pure tears
　　Our guilty spots away.

4 Mother of God! the sons of Eve
    Weeping, thine aid implore:
Oh! land us from the storms of life,
    Safe on th' eternal shore.

5 Glory, for graces manifold,
    To the one only Lord;
Whose mercy doth our souls forgive,
    Whose bounty doth reward.

119.   St. Francis.

1 LET Alverna's holy mountain
    That high mystery proclaim,
Of the stamps of life eternal
    Which on blessed Francis came;
While he sobb'd, and while he sighed,
Grieving for the Crucified.

2 There, within a lonely cavern,
    Far from all the world withdrawn,
As the Saint his watch was keeping,
    With incessant scourgings torn;
Ever musing more and more
On the wounds that Jesus bore;—

3 As he pray'd in cold and hunger;
    As he pour'd his glowing tears;
In his fervent spirit mounting
    Far above terrestrial spheres,
Every earthly thing forgot
In his Saviour's bitter lot;—

4 Lo to him, in form seraphic,
    Borne upon a cross on high,
Six irradiant wings expanding,
    Came the King of glory nigh!
Gazing on him with a face
Of benignity and grace.

He that tender glance returning,
  Saw th' Incarnate Light of Light;
Saw his gracious meek Redeemer,
  Rob'd in glory infinite;
Drank the words that from Him fell,—
Words divine, unspeakable!

6 Straightway all the sacred summit
    Kindles like a flaming pyre;
  Holy Francis sinks enraptur'd,
    Fainting with ecstatic fire;
  And upon his flesh appear
  Christ's immortal stigmata!

7 Honour to the high Redeemer,
    Who for us in torments died;
  In whose image blessed Francis
    Suffer'd and was sanctified,
  Counting every thing but loss
  For the glory of the Cross.

120. The Christmas Crib of St. Francis.

1 St. Francis kneels at Rome before the holy Father's chair,
  Who smiles upon his pious son, his earnest prayer receiving;
  Out in the open field, beneath heaven's star-lit ceiling fair,
  With Christmas jubilee to cheer the shepherds' hearts believing.

2 There, in the field at Greccia, in Reato's valley bright,
  For the first time St. Francis reared the crib we love so dearly;

With childlike thought, for childlike souls, that
    holy Christmas night,
He made the crib that now we come to kneel
    and pray at yearly.

Beside the crib the ox and ass are standing, still
    and mild;
The lantern glimmers in the cave, the holy scene
    revealing,—
The blessed Mother-Maiden; the little new-born
    Child;
And Joseph, and the shepherds, at the threshold
    meekly kneeling.

The herdsmen and the peasant-girls he taught to
    lift on high
Their hearts in pious hymns of praise, from lips
    that faintly falter;
While at the foot of that rude crib the priests
    are standing nigh,
The threefold Christmas Sacrifice to offer on the
    altar.

And thrice the holy Gospel that night St. Francis
    sang,
Nor yet the glowing words had ceased when morn-
    ing-dawn was waking.
Then all around, in hill and vale, the echo
    sweetly rang,
From soaring lark, and rustic flute, and shepherd-
    voices breaking.

Like a "Gloria in excelsis" the skylark's carol
    woke,
As from her wings she shook the dew in innocent
    oblation;
That "Gloria" which in ecstasy upon our Lady
    broke,
When the Light of Light smiled in her eyes, all
    lit with adoration.

7 Now, on the lips of priests and of simple shepherd-swains,
　The echo of that Gloria the saint's sweet skill is bringing,
　Which erst in Bethlehem's valley, in softly thrilling strains,
　To Jesus in the manger angelic tongues were singing.

8 And so St. Francis founded, in the days long past away,
　This jubilee of innocence, with childlike joy o'erflowing;
　Which kindles still, in our grave days, the Christmas candles gay,
　And the clear light of children's eyes with love and gladness glowing.

9 Now, with the angels beautiful, this blessed Christmas-tide,
　Sing, "Glory in the highest," to God the great and holy;
　With all "men of goodwill on earth" all peace and joy abide;
　And to the dear Child Jesus be adoration lowly!

---

121. Apostles and Evangelists.

1 Now let the earth with joy resound,
　And highest Heav'n re-echo round;
　Nor Heav'n nor earth too high can raise
　The great Apostles' glorious praise.

2 O ye who, thron'd in glory dread,
　Shall judge the living and the dead!
　Lights of the world for evermore!
　To you the suppliant prayer we pour.

3 Ye close the sacred gates on high;
  At your command apart they fly:
  Oh! loose us from the guilty chain
  We strive to break, and strive in vain.

4 Sickness and health your voice obey;
  At your command they go or stay:
  Oh, then from sin our souls restore;
  Increase our virtues more and more.

5 So when the world is at its end,
  And Christ to Judgment shall descend,
  May we be call'd those joys to see
  Prepar'd from all eternity.

6 Praise to the Father, with the Son,
  And Holy Spirit, Three in One;
  As ever was in ages past,
  And shall be so while ages last.

---

122.   2.

1 THE Lord's eternal gifts,
    Th' Apostles' mighty praise,
  Their victories, and high reward,
    Sing we in joyful lays.

2 Lords of the Churches they;
    Triumphant Chiefs of war;
  Brave Soldiers of the Heavenly Court;
    True lights for evermore.

3 Theirs was the Saints' high Faith;
    And quenchless Hope's pure glow;
  And perfect Charity, which laid
    The world's fell tyrant low.

4   In them the Father shone;
    In them the Son o'ercame;
  In them the Holy Spirit wrought,
    And fill'd their hearts with flame.

123. Hymn to the Four Evangelists.

1   From Sinai's trembling peak,
    In trumpet-blasts from Heaven,
  And thunders of a threat'ning God,
    The olden Law was given.

2   To us the selfsame Lord,
    Attemper'd to our gaze
  By the soft veil of flesh, Himself
    In love and grace displays.

3   On the hard rock engrav'd,
    The Law from Sinai's hill,
  Precepts supplied, but gave no strength
    Those precepts to fulfil.

4   Stamp'd in the heart, the Law
    Which Christ proclaim'd anew,
  With its commandment also gives
    The strength to will and do.

5   This Law with faithful pen
    Ye wrote, O Scribes of God;
  Preach'd it by holiest word and deed,
    And seal'd it with your blood.

6   Oh, may that Spirit blest,
    Who touch'd your lips with fire,
  Those same eternal words of life
    Deep in our hearts inspire!

124. For the Festival of a Bishop.

1 Jesu! Thy priests' eternal prize!
   This day on us look down—
This day, that saw Thee in the skies
   Thy holy Pontiff crown.

2 Chosen for his fidelity,
   His love, and prudence rare :
The sheep Thy Father gave to Thee,
   Thou gavest to his care.

3 He knew and lov'd them, each and all;
   Their lambs he gently led;
They, too, in turn obey'd his call,
   And in his footsteps fed.

4 Did any sheep the fold forsake,
   He sought it night and day;
And in his arm would bring it back,
   However rough the way.

5 He met the wolf's impetuous shock,
   His cunning wiles defied;
And for his flock—his own dear flock—
   Was ready to have died.

6 For them he offer'd with delight
   The Sacrifice ador'd;
Offering himself and his, with it,
   To his eternal Lord.

---

125. The Doctors of the Church.

1 O Thou, th' eternal Father's Word!
What though on earth Thy voice is heard
   No longer, as of yore;
Still, age by age, dost Thou supply
With holy teachers from on high
   Thy Church for evermore.

2 They, in Thy stead, the truth maintain,
   And guard the Christian Faith from stain
     Against its deadly foes;
  Which, under such protecting care,
  For ever fresh, for ever fair,
     In virgin beauty glows.

3 Remnants of superstition old,
   Falsehood and error, from the fold
     'Tis theirs to drive away;
  Theirs to recover to the Lord
  The souls, whom heresy and fraud
     Have made a wretched prey.

4 They, to the long hoar-headed line
   Of Fathers pointing, as they shine
     Far in the ages deep,
  Preserve the ancient doctrines pure;
  Confute the novel; and secure
     The great deposit keep.

5 All praise to Thee, who by the pen
   Of saintly doctors, teaching men
     Thy truths, O Truth sublime!
  Without a voice, without a sound,
  Thy grace diffusest all around,
     Thy glory through all time.

126. Festival of a Martyr.

1 MARTYR of unconquer'd might!
   Follower of th' eternal Son!
  Who, triumphant in the fight,
  Hast celestial glory won;

2 By the virtue of thy prayer,
   Wash our guilty stains away;
  Sin's contagion drive afar;
  Suffer not our feet to stray.

3 Loosen'd from the fleshly chain
　Which detain'd thee here of old,
Loose us from the bonds of sin,
　From the fetters of the world.

127.　　2.

1 SING we the Martyrs blest,
　Their blood for Jesus pour'd;
Sing we their glorious victories,
　And infinite reward.

2 Treading the world beneath,
　Spurning the body's pain,
'Twas theirs, in Martyrdom's brief space,
　Eternal joys to gain.

3 To raging flames consign'd,
　And ruthless beasts a prey;
Their sacred flesh by savage hooks
　Torn piece by piece away:

4 Their vitals hanging forth;—
　Unmov'd they still endure;
Unmov'd continue, in the grace
　Of endless life secure.

5 Saviour, to us vouchsafe,
　Of Thy dear clemency,
A portion with Thy Martyr Saints,
　Through all eternity.

128.　　3.

1 O THOU, the Martyrs' glorious King!
　Of Confessors the crown and prize!
Who dost to joys celestial bring
　Those who the joys of earth despise;

2 By all the praise Thy Saints have won;
   By all their pains in days gone by;
By all the deeds which they have done,—
   Hear Thou Thy suppliant people's cry.

3 Thou dost amid Thy Martyrs' fight;
   Thy Confessors Thou dost forgive;
May we find mercy in Thy sight,
   And in Thy sacred presence live.

129.   Virgins.

1 Thou Crown of all the Virgin choir!
   That holy Mother's Virgin Son!
Who is, alone of womankind,
   Mother and Virgin both in one!

2 Encircled by thy Virgin band,
   Amid the lilies thou art found;
For thy pure brides with lavish hand
   Scattering immortal graces round.

3 And still, wherever thou dost bend
   Thy lovely steps, O glorious King,
Virgins upon Thy steps attend,
   And hymns to Thy high glory sing.

4 Keep us, O Purity divine,
   From every least corruption free;
Our every sense from sin refine,
   And purify our souls for Thee.

5 To God the Father, and the Son,
   All honour, glory, praise, be given;
With Thee, O holy Paraclete!
   Henceforth by all in earth and Heaven.

130.   2.

1 O THOU Thy Mother's Maker, hail!
    Hail, Virgin-born! to Thee;
To-day a Virgin's death we sing,
    A Virgin's victory.

2 Oh, doubly blest! to whom was given
    Martyr and Virgin too,—
At once to triumph over death,
    And her frail sex subdue.

3 O'er fear, o'er thousand forms of pain,
    Victorious she stood;
And won the everlasting heights
    In streams of her own blood.

4 Oh, through her prayers our sins forgive,
    All good and gracious King:
So, purified in heart, may we
    Thy praise eternal sing.

---

131.   All Saints.

1 JERUSALEM, thou City blest!
Dear vision of celestial rest!
Which far above the starry sky,
Pil'd up with living stones on high,
Art, as a bride, encircled bright,
With million angel forms of light.

2 Thy gates a pearly lustre pour;
Thy gates are open evermore;
And thither evermore draw nigh
All who for Christ have dar'd to die;
Or, smit with love of their dear Lord,
Have pains endur'd and joys abhorr'd.

3 That House on high, it ever rings
With praises of the King of kings;
For ever there, on harps divine,
They hymn th' eternal One and Trine;
We here below the strain prolong,
And faintly echo Sion's song.

4 O Lord of lords invisible!
With Thy pure light this temple fill:
Hither, oft as invok'd, descend;
Here to thy people's prayer attend;
Here, through all hearts, for evermore
Thy Spirit's quick'ning graces pour.

5 Here may the faithful, day by day,
In kneeling adoration pray,
And here receive from Thy dear love
The blessings of that home above,
Till, loosen'd from this mortal chain,
Its everlasting joys they gain.

6 To God the Father, glory due
Be paid by all the heavenly host;
And to His only Son most true,
With Thee, O mighty Holy Ghost:
To whom praise, pow'r, and blessing be
Through ages of eternity.

132. Feast of All Saints.

1 O CHRIST, thy guilty people spare!
　Lo, kneeling at thy gracious throne,
Thy Virgin Mother pours her prayer,
　Imploring pardon for her own.

2 Ye Angels, happy evermore!
　Who in your circles nine ascend,
As ye have guarded us before,
　So still from harm our steps defend.

3 Ye Prophets, and Apostles high!
    Behold our penitential tears;
And plead for us when death is nigh,
    And our all-searching Judge appears.

4 Ye Martyrs all, a purple band,
    And Confessors, a white-robed train;
Oh, call us to our native land,
    From this our exile, back again!

5 And ye, O choirs of Virgins chaste!
    Receive us to your seats on high;
With Hermits whom the desert waste
    Sent up of old into the sky.

6 Drive from the flock, O Spirits blest!
    The false and faithless race away;
That all within one fold may rest,
    Secure beneath one Shepherd's sway.

---

33. Hymn for Sunday Morning.

1 AGAIN the Sunday morn
    Calls us to prayer and praise;
Waking our hearts to gratitude
    With its enlivening rays.

    But Christ yet brighter shone,
      Quenching the morning beam;
    When triumphing from death He rose,
      And rais'd us up with Him.

2 When first the world sprang forth,
  In majesty array'd,
And bath'd in streams of purest light;—
  What power was there display'd!

But oh, what love!—when Christ,
For our transgressions slain,
Was by th' Eternal Father rais'd
For us to life again.

3 His new-created world
The mighty Maker view'd,
With thousand lovely tints adorn'd;
And straight pronounc'd it good.

But oh! much more He joy'd
That self-same world to see
Wash'd in the Lamb's all-saving Blood
From its impurity.

4 Nature each day renews
Her beauty evermore;
Whence to God's hidden Majesty
The soul is taught to soar.

But Christ, the Light of all,
The Father's Image blest,
Gives us to see our God Himself
In Flesh made manifest.

134. For Vespers.

1 O BLEST Creator of the light!
Who dost the dawn from darkness bring;
And framing Nature's depth and height,
Didst with the new-born light begin;

2 Who gently blending eve with morn,
And morn with eve, didst call them day:—
Thick flows the flood of darkness down;
Oh, hear us as we weep and pray!

3 Keep Thou our souls from schemes of crime;
    Nor guilt remorseful let them know;
Nor, thinking but on things of time,
    Into eternal darkness go.

4 Teach us to knock at Heaven's high door;
    Teach us the prize of life to win;
Teach us all evil to abhor,
    And purify ourselves within.

135.   2.

1 Now doth the fiery sun decline :—
Thou, Unity Eternal! shine;
Thou, Trinity, Thy blessings pour,
And make our hearts with love run o'er.

2 Thee in the hymns of morn we praise;
To Thee our voice at eve we raise;
Oh, grant us, with Thy Saints on high,
Thee through all time to glorify.

3 Praise to the Father, with the Son,
And Holy Spirit, Three in One;
As ever was in ages past,
And shall be so while ages last.

136.   3.

1 O Thou the Father's Image blest!
    Who callest forth the morning ray;
  O Thou eternal Light of light,
    And inexhaustive Fount of day!

2 True Sun !—upon our souls arise,
  Shining in beauty evermore ;
And through each sense the quick'ning beam
  Of the eternal Spirit pour.

3 Thee too, O Father, we entreat,
  Father of might and grace divine !
Father of glorious majesty !
  Thy pitying eye on us incline.

4 Confirm us in each good resolve ;
  The Tempter's envious rage subdue ;
Turn each misfortune to our good ;
  Direct us right in all we do.

5 Rule Thou our inmost thoughts ; let no
  Impurity our hearts defile ;
Grant us a true and fervent faith ;
  Grant us a spirit free from guile.

6 May Christ Himself be our true Food,
  And Faith our daily cup supply ;
While from the Spirit's tranquil depth
  We drink unfailing draughts of joy.

7 Still ever with the peep of morn
  May saintly modesty attend ;
Faith sanctify the mid-day hours ;
  Upon the soul no night descend.

---

137. The Sign of the Cross.

1 O CHILD of God, remember,
  When thou to Christ wast born,
How then across thine infant breast
  His sacred Sign was drawn.

2 And when confirming chrism
   Upon thy brow was laid,
How in that Sign the Holy Ghost
   His grace upon thee shed.

3 Therefore, when sleep invites thee
   To take thy needful rest,
Be sure that with the sacred Cross
   Thou sign thy brow and breast.

4 The Cross hath wond'rous virtue
   All evil to control;
To scatter darkness, and to calm
   The tempest of the soul.

5 What though in sleep this body
   May helpless seem to lie;
I nothing fear; assur'd that One
   Stronger than all is nigh.

6 On Him my heart shall ponder,
   E'en while my rest I take;
My shield and shelter while I sleep;
   My joy when I awake.

138. Holy Relics.

1 Now, while before your relics
   Our prayers and incense rise,
Look down, ye Saints of Heaven!
   And help us from the skies.

2 What though in dismal ruin
   Your bones so long have lain,
Yet still sublimest virtues
   E'en in their dust remain:

3 Still in these holy temples
   The Spirit makes His home;
Reserving them for glory
   In ages yet to come:

4 Whence from beneath the altar
   They yet exert their might,
Subduing death and sickness,
   And putting Hell to flight.

5 O Christ, our Judge immortal,
   Through all the worlds, to Thee
All glory with the Father
   And Holy Spirit be.

139.   The Wanderer.

1 I WAS wandering and weary,
   When my Saviour came unto me;
For the ways of sin grew dreary,
   And the world had ceased to woo me:
And I thought I heard Him say,
As He came along His way,
     O silly Souls! come near Me;
     My sheep should never fear Me;
     I am the Shepherd true!

2 At first I would not hearken,
   And put off till the morrow;
But life began to darken,
   And I was sick with sorrow;
     And I thought I heard Him say, &c.

3 At last I stopped to listen,
   His voice could not deceive me;
I saw His kind eyes glisten,
   So anxious to relieve me:
     And I thought I heard Him say, &c.

4 He took me on His shoulder,
    And tenderly He kissed me;
He bade my love be bolder,
    And said how He had missed me;
        And I'm sure I heard Him say, &c.

5 Strange gladness seemed to move Him,
    Whenever I did better;
And He coaxed me so to love Him,
    As if He was my debtor;
        And I always heard Him say, &c.

6 I thought His love would weaken
    As more and more He knew me;
But it burneth like a beacon,
    And its light and heat go through me:
        And I ever hear Him say, &c.

7 Let us do, then, dearest brothers!
    What will best and longest please us;
Follow not the ways of others,
    But trust ourselves to Jesus;
        We shall ever hear Him say, &c.

140.   Trust.

1 Jesu, to Thee we look;
    Jesu, on Thee we call;
Jesu, extend Thy gentle crook,
    To save us when we fall.

2 A sheep by nature lost,
    An outcast here am I;
But Thou hast paid the dreadful cost,
    And wilt not pass me by.

3 Prayer is of faith the breath;
   It leads me, Lord, to Thee;
Thy death has been the death of Death,
   And Thou hast died for me.

4 Sweet Saviour, on the ground
   Thy face lies low in dust;
In seas of sorrow drenched and drowned,
   The Just for the unjust.

5 Seed of the Woman, Thou;
   By all our prayers and sighs,
To us Thy lowly suppliants now
   Reopen Paradise.

---

141. Dependence on Grace.

1 O LORD, behold a sinner kneel
   Before Thy gracious throne,
Confessing what he truly is,
   Left to himself alone.

2 Didst Thou remove the inward stay
   Of Thy supporting power,
No sin there is I might not do
   Within a single hour:

3 Or leaving me the grace I have,
   Didst Thou a moment cease
To curb those outward elements
   That war against my peace;

4 How quickly would my nature run
   The way temptation led;
Become to sin again alive,
   Again to virtue dead!

5 Within, without, I lean on Thee,
  On Thee for aid rely;
Oh, still my outward life protect,
  My inward life supply.

---

142. Faith.

1 O Gifts of gifts! O Grace of Faith!
  My God! how can it be
That Thou, who hast discerning love,
  Shouldst give that gift to me?

2 There was a place, there was a time,
  Whether by night or day,
Thy Spirit came and left that gift
  Upon His gracious way.

3 How many hearts Thou might'st have had
  More innocent than mine!
How many souls would less abuse
  That quick'ning Gift divine!

4 The crowd of cares, the weightiest cross,
  Seem trifles less than light;
Earth looks so little and so low,
  Where faith shines full and bright.

5 Oh, happy, happy that I am:
  If thou canst be, O Faith!
The treasure that thou art in life,
  What wilt thou be in death?

6 Thy choice, O God of Goodness, then
  I lovingly adore;
Oh, give me grace to keep Thy grace,
  And grace to merit more!

143.   Grace and Merit.

1 O Jesu, my beloved King!
   I give all thanks to Thee,
Who by Thy Cross hast merited
   Celestial grace for me.

2 In Adam, raised to dignities
   Transcendent and divine;
In Adam, fallen from the bliss
   That once in him was mine:

3 That grace to which my native strength
   Could never have attain'd,
That grace, O my Incarnate God,
   In Thee I have regain'd.

4 O gift of love! O gift immense!
   Surpassing nature's law!
What strength to will and to perform
   From this pure fount I draw!

5 By this, how many passing acts
   Which else had been in vain,
Endued with meritorious power,
   A prize eternal gain!

6 By this, to me is open'd wide,
   Through death's inviting door,
A brighter realm, a nobler crown,
   Than Adam lost of yore.

7 O Jesu, on whose grace alone
   I by Thy grace depend;
Grant me the grace to persevere
   In grace unto the end!

144. Self-Examination.

1 OH, wouldst thou learn, poor self,
    The evil thou hast done,
  First thy corrupt propensities
    Examine, one by one;

2 And next, consider well
    How freely, day by day,
  Thou hast pursued them, each in turn,
    Where'er they led the way.

3 Thus shalt thou find thy sins
    To be in number more
  Than all the hairs upon thy head,
    Or sands upon the shore.

4 Thus shall the Lord to thee
    Thy miseries disclose;
  Oh, happy, if thou seek betimes
    The remedy He shows!

145. The End of my Creation.

1 OFT, my soul, thyself remind
  Of the end thy God designed
  When He sent thee here on earth,
  Heir of an immortal birth.

2 Ah, what else did He desire,
  Save in graces to attire,
  Then to crown with glory bright,
  Thee the child of His delight?

3 Learn, O spirit, learn to know
  This thy single end below;
  Learn by this alone to weigh
  All the passing world's display

4 Whatsoe'er this end obscures;
Whatsoe'er from it allures;
What impedes it, or belies,
Sever from thee, timely wise.

5 Every moment, day and night,
Keep it clearly in thy sight;
If thou hope, o'ercoming sin,
Joys of endless life to win.

146. Thanksgiving for my Creation.

1 NOT, Lord, by any will of mine,
   But of Thy gracious plan,
Father eternal and divine,
   My earthly life began.

2 By Thy election from a state
   Of nothingness I came;
Thy hand my spirit did create,
   And my corporeal frame.

3 As now I live and draw my breath
   In Thee, O God most high;
So, too, to Thee I look in death
   For immortality.

4 On Thee, through every future scene
   Of being, I depend;
Thou, my beginning, Lord, hast been,
   Thou also art my end.

147. The Yoke of Christ.

1 CHRISTIAN soul, dost thou desire
   Days of joy, and peace, and truth?
Learn to bear the yoke of Jesus
   In the spring-tide of thy youth.

2 It may seem at first a burden;
   But thy Lord will make it light;
   He Himself will bear it with thee;
   He will ease thee of its weight.

3 Only bear it well; and daily
   Thou wilt learn that yoke to love;
   Strength and grace it here will bring thee,
   And a bright reward above.

148.   Jesus.

1 Jesus, my Saviour, my God, my Friend,
   In life and in death my soul defend;
   In joy and in sorrow, in good and ill,
   Be Thou my Guide and Protector still.

2 My joy, Thy glory; my hope, Thy Name,
   Most loving Jesus, my heart inflame:
   Grant I may never desert Thy Side;
   Sorrowing Jesus, be Thou my Guide.

3 Let not Thy sorrows and sighs be vain,
   Suffering Jesus, my soul sustain;
   Since Thou didst weep in Thy mortal years,
   Crucified Jesus, accept my tears.

4 When in affliction and grief I bend,
   Comforting Jesus, be Thou my friend:
   To Thee I fly, as a sure repose;
   Conquering Jesus, subdue my foes.

5 In the paths of peace all my steps direct,
   Powerful Jesus, my soul protect;
   Grant I may walk in Thy footsteps bright,
   Glorious Jesus, be Thou my light.

6 When my race is run, and I reach the goal,
Merciful Jesus, accept my soul:
Freed from all sorrow, and tears, and woe,
Bountiful Jesus, my crown bestow.

149. Faith of our Fathers.

1 FAITH of our Fathers! living still,
   In spite of dungeon, fire, and sword:
Oh, how our hearts beat high with joy
   Whene'er we hear that glorious word:
Faith of our Fathers! Holy Faith!
We will be true to thee till death!

2 Our Fathers, chained in prisons dark,
   Were still in heart and conscience free:
How sweet would be their children's fate,
   If they, like them, could die for thee!
     Faith of our Fathers, &c.

3 Faith of our Fathers! Mary's prayers
   Shall win our country back to thee;
And through the truth that comes from God,
   England shall then indeed be free.
     Faith of our Fathers, &c.

4 Faith of our Fathers! we will love
   Both friend and foe in all our strife:
And preach thee too, as love knows how,
   By kindly words and virtuous life.
     Faith of our Fathers, &c.

150. THE SAME.—FOR IRELAND.

1 FAITH of our Fathers! living still,
    In spite of dungeon, fire, and sword:
Oh! Ireland's hearts beat high with joy
    Whene'er they hear that glorious word,
Faith of our Fathers! Holy Faith!
We will be true to thee till death!

2 Our Fathers, chained in prisons dark,
    Were still in heart and conscience free:
How sweet would be their children's fate,
    If they, like them, could die for thee!
        Faith of our Fathers, &c.

3 Faith of our Fathers! Mary's prayers
    Shall keep our country fast to thee;
And through the truth that comes from God,
    Oh, we shall prosper and be free!
        Faith of our Fathers, &c.

4 Faith of our Fathers! we must love
    Both friend and foe in all our strife;
And preach thee too, as love knows how,
    By kindly words and virtuous life.
        Faith of our Fathers, &c.

5 Faith of our Fathers! guile and force
    To do thee bitter wrong unite;
But Erin's Saints shall fight for us,
    And keep undimmed thy blessed light.
        Faith of our Fathers, &c.

6 Faith of our Fathers! distant shores
    Their happy faith to Ireland owe;
Then in our home, oh, shall we not
    Break the dark plots against thee now?
        Faith of our Fathers, &c.

7 Faith of our Fathers! days of old
   Within our hearts speak gallantly:
For ages thou hast stood by us,
   Dear Faith! and now we'll stand by thee.
     Faith of our Fathers, &c.

151. The Pilgrims of the Night.

1 Hark, hark, my soul! angelic songs are swelling
   O'er earth's green fields and ocean's wave-beat shore!
How sweet the truth those blessed strains are telling
   Of that new life when sin shall be no more!
      Angels of Jesus!
      Angels of light!
     Singing to welcome
     The pilgrims of the night.

2 Darker than night life's shadows fall around us,
   And, like benighted men, we miss our mark;
God hides Himself, and grace hath scarcely found us,
   Ere death finds out his victims in the dark.
     Angels of Jesus! &c.

3 Onward we go, for still we hear them singing,
   Come, weary souls! for Jesus bids you come!
And through the dark, its echoes sweetly ringing,
   The music of the Gospel leads us home.
     Angels of Jesus! &c.

4 Far, far away, like bells at evening pealing,
   The voice of Jesus sounds o'er land and sea,
And laden souls, by thousands meekly stealing,
   Kind Shepherd! turn their weary steps to Thee.
     Angels of Jesus! &c.

5 Rest comes at length, though life be long and
  dreary;
 The day must dawn, and darksome night be
  past;
All journeys end in welcomes to the weary,
 And heaven, the heart's true home, will come
  at last.
    Angels of Jesus! &c.

6 Cheer up, my soul! faith's moonbeams softly
  glisten
 Upon the breast of life's most troubled sea;
And it will cheer thy drooping heart to listen
 To those brave songs which angels mean for
  thee.
    Angels of Jesus! &c.

7 Angels! sing on, your faithful watches keeping,
 Sing us sweet fragments of the songs above;
While we toil on, and soothe ourselves with weep-
  ing,
 Till life's long night shall break in endless love.
    Angels of Jesus!
     Angels of light!
    Singing to welcome
     The pilgrims of the night.

---

152. The Christian's Song on his March to Heaven.

1 BLEST is the Faith, divine and strong,
 Of thanks and praise an endless fountain,
Whose life is one perpetual song,
 High up the Saviour's holy mountain.
  Oh, Sion's songs are sweet to sing
   With melodies of gladness laden;
  Hark! how the harps of angels ring,
   Hail, Son of Man! hail, Mother-Maiden!

2 Blest is the hope that holds to God
  In doubt and darkness still unshaken,
And sings along the heavenly road
  Sweetest when most it seems forsaken.
    Oh, Sion's songs, &c.

3 Blest is the love that cannot love
  Aught that earth gives of best and brightest;
Whose raptures thrill, like saints' above,
  Most when its earthly gifts are lightest.
    Oh, Sion's songs, &c.

4 Blest is the penance that believes
  That charity turns hell to heaven;
Counts its dark sins, and while it grieves
  Hopes for all that to be forgiven.
    Oh, Sion's songs, &c.

5 Blest is the time that in the eye
  Of God its hopeful watch is keeping,
And grows into eternity
  Like noiseless trees when men are sleeping.
    Oh, Sion's songs, &c.

6 Blest is the death that good men die,
  Solemn, self-doubting, firm, and wary;
Trusting to God its destiny,
  And leaning for its hour on Mary.
    Oh, Sion's songs, &c.

153. Fight for Sion.

1 CHRISTIANS! to the war!
  Gather from afar!
    Hark! hark! the word is given;
  Jesus bids us fight
  "For God and the Right,"
    And for Mary, the Queen of Heaven!

Now first for thee, thou wicked world!
  Puffed up with godless pomp and pageant!
Avenging grace to humble thee
  Can make the weakest arm its agent.
    Christians! to the war!
    Gather from afar!
      Hark! hark! the word is given;
    Jesus bids us fight
    "For God and the Right,"
      And for Mary, the Queen of Heaven!

2 And thou, dark fiend, six thousand years
    The Bride of Christ in vain tormenting,
  Shalt find our hate and scorn of thee
    Deep as thine own, and unrelenting.
      Christians! to the war, &c.

3 Ah! Self! so oft forgiven, thou
    Canst play no part but that of traitor.
  We spare thy life; but thou must bear
    The felon's brand, the captive's fetter.
      Christians! to the war, &c.

4 But worse than devil, flesh, or world,
    Human respect, like poison creeping,
  Chills and unnerves the hosts of Christ,
    When weary war-worn hearts are sleeping.
      Christians! to the war, &c.

5 Like lions roaring for their prey,
    Armies of foes are round us trooping;
  What then? see! countless angels come
    To heal the hurt, to raise the drooping.
      Christians! to the war, &c.

6 Then bravely, comrades, to the fight,
    With shout and song each other cheering;
  Strength not our own from heaven descends,
    The sun breaks out, the clouds are clearing.
      Christians! to the war, &c.

7 On to the gates of Sion, on!
    Break through the foe with fresh endeavour;
We'll hang our colours up in heaven,
    When peace shall be proclaimed for ever.
    Christians! to the war, &c.

154.   An Evening Hymn.

1 SWEET Saviour! bless us ere we go;
    Thy word into our minds instil;
And make our lukewarm hearts to glow
    With lowly love and fervent will.
Through life's long day and death's dark night,
O gentle Jesus! be our light!

2 The day is done, its hours have run;
    And Thou hast taken count of all,—
The scanty triumphs grace hath won,
    The broken vow, the frequent fall.
    Through life's long day, &c.

3 Grant us, dear Lord! from evil ways
    True absolution and release;
And bless us more than in past days
    With purity and inward peace.
    Through life's long day, &c.

4 Do more than pardon; give us joy,
    Sweet fear and sober liberty;
And simple hearts without alloy,
    That only long to be like Thee.
    Through life's long day, &c.

5 Labour is sweet, for Thou hast toiled;
    And care is light, for Thou hast cared:
Ah! never let our works be soiled
    With strife, or by deceit ensnared.
    Through life's long day, &c.

6 For all we love, the poor, the sad,
    The sinful,—unto Thee, we call;
Oh, let Thy mercy make us glad:
    Thou art our Jesus and our All!
        Through life's long day, &c.

---

155.   Morning.

1 Now doth the sun ascend the sky,
    And wake creation with its ray:
Be present with us, Lord most high,
    Through all the actions of the day.

2 Keep us, eternal Lord, this day
    From every sinful passion free;
Grant us in all we do and say,
    In all our thoughts, to honour Thee.

3 So when the evening stars appear,
    And in their train the darkness bring,
May we, O Lord, with conscience clear,
    To Thee our grateful praises sing.

4 To God the Father glory be,
    And to his sole-begotten Son;
The same, O Holy Ghost, to Thee,
    While everlasting ages run.

---

156.   2.

1 O LORD, of perfect purity,
    Who dost the world with light adorn,
And paint the fields of azure sky
    With lovely hues of eve and morn;

2 Upon our fainting souls distil
   The grace of Thy celestial dew;
Let no fresh snare to sin beguile,
   No former sin revive anew.

3 Keep Thou our souls from schemes of crime,
   No guilt remorseful let them know;
Nor, thinking but on things of time,
   Into eternal darkness go.

4 Teach us to knock at heaven's high door,
   Teach us the prize of life to win;
Teach us all evil to abhor,
   And purify ourselves within.

5 Be Thou our guide, be Thou our goal,
   Be Thou our pathway to the skies;
Our joy when sorrow fills the soul,
   In death our everlasting prize.

6 To God the Father glory be,
   And to His sole-begotten Son;
The same, O Holy Ghost, to Thee,
   While everlasting ages run.

157.   Evening.

1 The sun is sinking fast;
   The daylight dies;
Let love awake and pay
   Her evening sacrifice.

2 As Christ upon the Cross
   In death reclin'd,
Into His Father's hands
   His parting soul resign'd;

3 So now herself my soul
    Would wholly give
Into His sacred charge,
    In whom all spirits live:

4 So now beneath His eye
    Would calmly rest,
Without a wish or thought
    Abiding in the breast.

5 Save that His will be done,
    Whate'er betide;
Dead to herself, and dead
    In Him to all beside.

6 Thus would I live;—yet now
    Not I, but He;
In all His power and love
    Henceforth alive in me!

7 One sacred Trinity!
    One Lord divine!
Myself for ever His!
    And He for ever mine!

158.   2.

1 Now with the fast-departing light,
    Maker of all! we ask of Thee,
Of Thy great mercy through the night
    Our guardian and defence to be.

2 Far off let idle visions fly;
    No phantom of the night molest:
Curb Thou our raging enemy,
    That we in chaste repose may rest.

3 Father of mercies, hear our cry!
   Hear us, O sole-begotten Son!
  Who, with the Holy Ghost most high,
   Reignest while endless ages run.

159. Prayer of St. Ignatius.

1 I LOVE, I love Thee, Lord most high!
   Because Thou first hast lovèd me;
  I seek no other liberty
   But that of being bound to Thee.

2 May memory no thought suggest,
   But shall to Thy pure glory tend;
  My understanding find no rest
   Except in Thee, its only end.

3 My God, I here protest to Thee,
   No other will have I than Thine;
  Whatever Thou hast giv'n to me,
   I here again to Thee resign.

4 All mine is Thine,—say but the word;
   Whate'er Thou willest shall be done:
  I know Thy love, all-gracious Lord;
   I know it seeks my good alone.

5 Apart from Thee all things are naught;
   Then grant, O my supremest bliss,
  Grant me to love Thee as I ought;
   Thou givest all in giving this!

160. Hymn of St. Francis Xavier.

1 MY God, I love Thee, not because
   I hope for heav'n thereby;
  Nor because they who love Thee not
   Must burn eternally.

2 Thou, O my Jesus, Thou didst me
   Upon the Cross embrace;
For me didst bear the nails and spear,
   And manifold disgrace;

3 And griefs and torments numberless,
   And sweat of agony;
E'en death itself;—and all for one
   Who was Thine enemy.

4 Then why, O blessed Jesu Christ!
   Should I not love Thee well;
Not for the sake of winning Heaven,
   Or of escaping hell:

5 Not with the hope of gaining aught;
   Not seeking a reward;
But, as Thyself hast loved me,
   O ever-loving Lord?

6 Ev'n so I love Thee, and will love,
   And in Thy praise will sing;
Solely because Thou art my God,
   And my eternal King.

---

161. Hymn to the Holy Cross.

1 HAIL to thee, blessed Rood!
   Conqueror of death! on thee
My Saviour, King, and God
   Hung in His agony.

2 Thou art the Queen of Trees,
   The medicine of Salvation;
When cares oppress, our ease;
   In grief, our consolation.

3 Oh, our Salvation's sign,
   Thou ever-blessed Rood!
Thou bearest Fruit divine,—
   Jesus, the sinner's food!

4 When they who hate, and they
   Who love, Thy Cross shall be
Summoned, that awful day,
   Thou Son of God, by Thee,
O Jesus, then, I pray,
   In mercy think of me!

---

162. "O Deus, ego amo Te."

1 I LOVE Thee, O my God, my Lord,
And not for hope of Thy reward
   Of bliss above,
And not for fear of endless woes,
And endless torments due to those
   Who slight Thy love.

2 Didst Thou for me the Cross embrace?
Alas! the shame, the sore disgrace,
   I've brought on Thee!
O lance! O nails! O thorny wreath!
O cruel pains, endured till death,
   And all for me!

3 'Twas love, O Jesus, made Thee mine,
And love, my God, shall make me Thine;
   Then, Jesus, then,
Thee will I love and Thee adore,
My King, my Lord, for evermore.
   Amen, amen.

163. School Hymn.

1 O Jesus! God and Man!
   For love of children once a child!
O Jesus! God and Man!
   We hail Thee Saviour sweet and mild!

2 O Jesus! God and Man!
   Make us poor children dear to Thee,
And lead us to Thyself,
   To love Thee for eternity.

3 O Mary! Mother-Maid!
   God made thee Mother of the poor!
Mary! to thee we look,
   To make our souls' salvation sure.

4 O Mary! Mother dear!
   Thank God, for us, for all His love;
And pray that in our faith
   We all may true and steadfast prove.

5 O Jesus! Mary's Son!
   On Thee for grace we children call;
Make us all men to love,
   But to love Thee beyond them all.

6 O Jesus! bless our work,
   Our sorrows soothe, our sins forgive;
O happy, happy they
   Who in the Church of Jesus live!

7 O God, most great and good,
   At work or play, by night or day,
Make us remember Thee,
   Who dost remember us alway!

164. Hymn for a Happy Death.

1 Jesus! ever-loving Saviour,
　　Thou didst live and die for me
　Living I will live to love Thee,
　　Dying I will die for Thee.
　　　　Jesus! Jesus!
　By Thy life and death of sorrow,
　　Help me in my agony.

2 When the last dread hour approaching
　　Fills my guilty soul with fear,
　All my sins rise up before me,
　　All my virtues disappear.
　　　　Jesus! Jesus!
　Turn not Thou in anger from me;
　　Mary! Joseph! then be near.

3 Kindest Jesus! Thou wert standing
　　By Thy foster-father's bed,
　While Thy Mother softly praying,
　　Held her dying Joseph's head.
　　　　Jesus! Jesus!
　By that death so calm and holy,
　　Soothe me in the hour of dread.

4 Mary! Thou canst not forsake me,
　　Virgin Mother undefiled!
　Thou didst not abandon Jesus,
　　Dying tortured and reviled.
　　　　Jesus! Jesus!
　Send Thy Mother to console me;—
　　Mary! help thy guilty child.

5 Jesus! when in cruel anguish
　　Dying on the shameful Tree,
　All abandon'd by Thy Father,
　　Thou didst writhe in agony.
　　　　Jesus! Jesus!
　By those three long hours of sorrow
　　Thou didst purchase hope for me.

6 When the priest with holy unction
    Prays for mercy and for grace,
May the tears of deep compunction
    All my guilty stains efface.
      Jesus! Jesus!
Let me find in Thee a refuge,
    In Thy heart a resting-place.

7 Oh, by all that Thou didst suffer,
    Grant me mercy in that day!
Help me, Mary, my sweet Mother!
    Holy Joseph, near me stay!
      Jesus! Jesus!
Let me die my lips repeating,
    Jesus, mercy! Mary, pray!

165.   Purgatory.

1 HELP, Lord, the souls which Thou hast made,
    The souls to Thee so dear,
In prison for the debt unpaid
    Of sins committed here.

2 Those holy souls, they suffer on,
    Resigned in heart and will,
Until Thy high behest is done,
    And justice has its fill.

3 For daily falls, for pardoned crime,
    They joy to undergo
The shadow of Thy Cross sublime,
    The remnant of Thy woe.

4 Help, Lord, the souls which Thou hast made,
    The souls to Thee so dear,
In prison for the debt unpaid
    Of sins committed here.

5 Oh, by their patience of delay,
   Their hope amid their pain,
Their sacred zeal to burn away
   Disfigurement and stain;

6 Oh, by their fire of love, not less
   In keenness than the flame,
Oh, by their very helplessness,
   Oh, by Thy own great Name,

7 Sweet Jesu, help, sweet Jesu, aid,
   The souls to Thee so dear,
In prison for the debt unpaid
   Of sins committed here!

166. "Dies iræ, dies illa."

1 Day of wrath! the heart dismaying,
High the bannered Cross displaying,
O'er the world in flames decaying.

2 Oh, what dread and bitter crying
Shall there be when, all things trying,
Comes the Judge, the All-descrying!

3 Through the tombs of nations swelling
Thrills the trump, of judgment telling,
All before the throne compelling.

4 Death and time in consternation
Then shall stand; while all Creation
Rises at that dread citation.

5 Lo! the open Book is giving
Witness sure to dead and living,
And the world its doom receiving.

6 Then the Judge shall sit, revealing
Every hidden thought and feeling,
Unto each requital dealing.

7 Who will aid me, interceding,
   For a wretched sinner pleading,
   When the just all grace are needing?

8 Heavenly King of dreadful splendour!
   Fount of love and pity tender!
   Be my Saviour and Defender.

9 Jesus! think for my salvation
   Thou didst quit Thy heavenly station;
   Leave me not to condemnation!

10 Weary, didst Thou seek me straying,
   On the cross my ransom paying;
   By Thy passion, hear my praying.

11 God of justice, my petition
   Hear, and grant my sins' remission,
   In that awful day's decision.

12 Shame and grief my soul oppressing,
   I bewail my life's transgressing,
   Hear me, Lord, my sins confessing!

13 Thou didst spare the sinner grieving,
   Thou didst save the thief believing,
   Me too hope of pardon giving.

14 Worthless are my prayers and mourning,
   Yet, good Lord, in pity yearning,
   Save me from the endless burning.

15 With the sheep assign my station
   On Thy right hand of salvation,
   At that awful separation.

16 When the lost are driven before Thee
   To their condemnation worthy,
   Call me with Thy Saints to glory.

17 Conscious guilt my spirit lading,
   Hear Thou, Lord, my self-upbraiding,
   Come—in death Thy suppliant aiding.

18 Oh, that day of tears and trembling,
   From the wreck of worlds assembling,

19 Sinners stand, their doom receiving,
   Spare them, God of dead and living!

20 Lord of mercy, Jesu blest!
   Grant them everlasting rest.
                              Amen.

---

167. Hymn for Confirmation.

1 SIGNED with the Cross that Jesus bore,
  We kneel, and tremblingly adore
     Our King upon His throne.
  The lights upon the altar shine
  Around His Majesty divine,
     Our God and Mary's Son.

2 Now, in that Presence dread and sweet,
  His own dear Spirit we entreat
     Who sevenfold gifts hath shed
  On us, who fall before Him now,
  Bearing the Cross upon our brow
     On which our Master bled.

3 Spirit of Wisdom! turn our eyes
  From earth and earthly vanities,
     To heavenly truth and love.
  Spirit of understanding true!
  Our souls with heavenly light endue
     To seek the things above.

4 Spirit of Counsel! be our guide;
   Teach us, by earthly struggles tried,
      Our heavenly crown to win.
   Spirit of fortitude! Thy power
   Be with us in temptation's hour,
      To keep us pure from sin.

5 Spirit of knowledge! lead our feet
   In Thine own paths so safe and sweet,
      By angel footsteps trod;
   Where Thou our Guardian true shalt be,
   Spirit of gentle piety,
      To keep us close to God.

6 But most of all, be ever near,
   Spirit of God's most holy fear!
      In our hearts' inmost shrine:
   Our souls with awful reverence fill,
   To worship His most holy Will,
      All-righteous and divine.

7 So, dearest Lord, through peace or strife,
   Lead us to everlasting life,
      Where only rest may be.
   What matter where our lot is cast,
   If only it may end at last
      With Mary and with Thee!

---

168. Renewal of Baptismal Vows.

1 O FATHER, Son, and Holy Ghost,
     One God in Persons three,
   We come in faith to count the cost,
     And give ourselves to Thee.

2 In hope and love Thy name we bless
   For countless mercies given;
To make our earthly burdens less,
   And smooth our way to heaven.

3 But most we thank Thee for the grace
   Of that thrice-blessed day
Which sped us in our Christian race,
   And washed our sin away.

4 *Then* we were free from guilty stain,
   But sad and sinful *now;*
With contrite hearts we come again
   To make our solemn vow.

5 Dear Lord, before Thy wounded Feet
   Weeping Thy children fall:
Hear us, kind Jesus, Saviour sweet,
   Our Life, our Love, our All.

6 We seek to serve no other king,
   Follow no other guide,
Nor earth, nor any earthly thing
   Shall tear us from Thy side.

7 We seek to know no other love,
   Save what we love in Thee;
And Thee we choose all else above
   Our chiefest Love to be.

8 Thy Blood our only treasure is,
   Thy Cross our chosen part;
Thyself and Mary all our bliss,
   Our home, Thy sacred Heart.

169. My Jesus, say.

1 My Jesus, say what wretch has dared
　Thy sacred hands to bind?
And who has dared to buffet so
　Thy face so meek and kind?
　　'Tis I have thus ungrateful been,
　　　Yet, Jesus, pity take;
　　Oh, spare and pardon me, my Lord,
　　　For Thy sweet mercy's sake.
　　　　[In singing, this verse may be repeated after
　　　　　each stanza but the last.]

2 My Jesus, who with spittle vile
　Profaned Thy sacred brow?
Or whose unpitying scourge has made
　Thy precious blood to flow?

3 My Jesus, whose the hands that wove
　That cruel thorny crown?
Who made that hard and heavy cross
　That weighs Thy shoulders down?

4 My Jesus, who has mock'd thy thirst
　With vinegar and gall?
Who held the nails that pierced Thy hands,
　And made the hammer fall?

5 My Jesus, say who dared to nail
　Those tender feet of Thine;
And whose the arm that raised the lance
　To pierce that heart divine?

6 And, Mary, who has murder'd thus
　Thy loved and only One?
Canst thou forgive the blood-stain'd hand
　That robb'd thee of thy Son?
　　'Tis I have thus ungrateful been
　　　To Jesus and to thee;
　　Forgive me for thy Jesus' sake,
　　　And pray to Him for me.

170. Paraphrase of St. Ignatius's Hymn, "Anima Jesu Christi."

1 Soul of Jesus, make me holy,
Make me contrite, meek, and lowly;
Soul most stainless, Soul divine,
Cleanse this sordid soul of mine;
Hallow this polluted soul,
Purify it, make it whole;—
Soul of Jesus! hallow me:
Miserere Domine!

2 Save me, Body of my Lord!
Save a sinner vile, abhorred.
Sacred Body, wan and worn,
Bruised and mangled, crushed and torn,
Piercèd Hands, and Feet, and Side,
Scourged, insulted, crucified,—
Save me! to the Cross I flee:
Miserere Domine!

3 Blood of Jesus! Stream of life,
Sacred stream with blessing rife,
From Thy broken Body shed
On the Cross, that Altar dread,—
Blood most precious, Fount divine,—
Fill my heart and make it Thine.
Blood of Christ! my cleansing be:
Miserere Domine!

4 Holy Water! Stream that poured
From Thy wounded Side, dear Lord,
Wash Thou me; without, within,
Cleanse me from the stain of sin,
Till my soul is clean and white,
Bathed, and purified, and bright
As a ransomed soul should be:
Miserere Domine!

5 Jesus! by the wondrous power
Of Thine awful Passion-hour,
By the unimagined woe
Mortal man may never know,
By the Cross upon Thee laid,
By the ransom Thou hast paid
By Thy passion, comfort me:
Miserere Domine!

6 Jesus! by Thy bitter death,
By Thy last expiring breath,
Give me the eternal life
Won in that tremendous strife.
Thou didst suffer death that I
Might not die eternally:
By Thy dying quicken me:
Miserere Domine!

7 Miserere! let me be
Never parted, Lord, from Thee;
Guard me from my ruthless foe,
Save me from eternal woe.
In the dreadful Judgment-day
Be Thy cross my hope and stay:
When the hour of death is near,
And my spirit faints for fear,
Call me with Thy voice of love,
Place me near to Thee above,
With Thine angel-hosts to raise
Never-ending hymns of praise!

171. Life Eternal.

1 LIFE eternal! Life eternal!
   Words that pierce the heart with fire!
Life eternal! Life eternal!
   How my soul doth thee desire!

2 Life eternal! Life eternal!
   Hope of hopes to mortal man!
Life eternal! Life eternal!
   I will grasp thee if I can.

3 Life eternal! Life eternal!
   Depth of depth of bliss unknown!
Life eternal! Life eternal!
   Thee I seek in Christ alone.

172.   Heaven.

1 O HEAVENLY Jerusalem,
   Of everlasting halls,
Thrice blessed are the people
   Who live within Thy walls.

2 Thou art the golden mansion,
   Where saints for ever sing;
The seat of God's own chosen,
   The palace of the King.

3 There God for ever sitteth,
   Himself of all the crown;
The Lamb the light that shineth,
   And never goeth down.

4 Naught to this seat approacheth,
   Their sweet peace to molest;
They sing their God for ever,
   Nor day nor night they rest.

5 To Christ, the Son that lightens
   His Church, above, below;
To Father and to Spirit
   Let things created bow.

APPENDIX.

173. Hymn to St. Patrick.

1 Hail, glorious St. Patrick, dear saint of our isle!
On us, thy poor children, bestow a sweet smile;
And now thou art high in thy mansions above,
On Erin's green valleys look down in thy love.

2 Hail, glorious St. Patrick! thy words were once strong
Against Satan's wiles and a heretic throng;
Not less is thy might where in heaven thou art:
Oh, come to our aid, in our battle take part!

3 In the war against sin, in the fight for the faith,
Dear saint, may thy children resist to the death;
May their strength be in meekness, in penance and prayer,
Their banner the cross, which they glory to bear.

4 Thy people, now exiles on many a shore,
Shall love and revere thee till time be no more;
And the fire thou hast kindled shall ever burn bright,
Its warmth undiminished, undying its light.

5 Ever bless and defend the sweet land of our birth,
Where the shamrock still blooms as when thou wert on earth;
And our hearts shall yet burn wheresoever we roam,
For God and St. Patrick and our native home.

174. The Sacred Heart.

1 I rise from dreams of time,
From the shadows of this life,
From the tombs and places waste,
From an earth of sin and strife;
I rise from dreams of time,
And an angel guides my feet
To the sacred altar-throne
Whereon Thy Heart doth beat.

2 The lone lamp quivers still,
And a wondrous silence reigns,
Only with low voice mild
The Holy One complains:
"Long I have waited here,
And though thou heed'st not me,
The Heart of Mary's Son
Beats ever on for thee."

3 In the womb of maiden meek,
In the cradle, on the tree,
Heart of undying love,
It lived, loved, broke for me:
While around me thunders peal,
Yet as then behold me now,
By Thy pierced and wounded Hands,
By Thy torn and bleeding Brow.

4 O voice of the inward ear!
O voice of complaining love!
O Thou that art awful God!
To realms below and above,
Thou waitest and pleadest here,
And can'st not from us part,
O veiled and wondrous Son!
O love of the Sacred Heart!

175. The Infant Jesus.

1 DEAR Little One! how sweet Thou art,
  Thine eyes how bright they shine,
So bright, they almost seem to speak
  When Mary's look meets Thine!

2 How faint and feeble is Thy cry,
  Like plaint of harmless dove,
When Thou dost murmur in Thy sleep
  Of sorrow and of love!

3 When Mary bids Thee sleep Thou sleep'st,
  Thou wakest when she calls;
Thou art content upon her lap,
  Or in the rugged stalls.

4 Simplest of Babes! with what a grace
  Thou dost Thy Mother's will!
Thine infant fashions well betray
  The Godhead's hidden skill.

5 When Joseph takes Thee in His arms,
  And smooths Thy little cheek,
Thou lookest up into his face
  So helpless and so meek.

6 Yes! Thou art what Thou seem'st to be,
  A thing of smiles and tears;
Yet Thou art God, and heaven and earth
  Adore Thee with their fears.

7 Yes! dearest Babe! those tiny hands,
  That play with Mary's hair,
The weight of all the mighty world
  This very moment bear.

8 Art Thou, weak Babe, my very God?
  Oh, I must love Thee then,
Love Thee, and yearn to spread Thy love
  Among forgetful men!

176. Thanksgiving after Communion.

1 Jesus, gentlest Saviour!
    God of might and power!
Thou Thyself art dwelling
    In us at this hour.

2 Nature cannot hold Thee,
    Heaven is all too strait
For Thine endless glory
    And Thy royal state.

3 Out beyond the shining
    Of the furthest star,
Thou art ever stretching
    Infinitely far.

4 Yet the hearts of children
    Hold what worlds cannot,
And the God of wonders
    Loves the lowly spot.

5 As men to their gardens
    Go to seek sweet flowers,
In our hearts dear Jesus
    Seeks them at all hours.

6 Jesus, gentlest Saviour!
    Thou art in us now;
Fill us full of goodness
    Till our hearts o'erflow.

7 Pray the prayer within us
    That to heaven shall rise;
Sing the song that angels
    Sing above the skies.

8 Multiply our graces,
    Chiefly love and fear,
And, dear Lord! the chiefest—
    Grace to persevere.

9 Oh, how can we thank Thee
    For a gift like this,
  Gift that truly maketh
    Heaven's eternal bliss?

10 Ah! when wilt Thou always
    Make our hearts Thy home?
  We must wait for heaven,—
    Then the day will come.

11 Now at least we'll keep Thee
    All the time we may;
  But Thy grace and blessing
    We will keep alway.

12 When our hearts Thou leavest,
    Worthless though they be,
  Give them to Thy Mother
    To be kept for Thee.

177. Immaculate! Immaculate!

THE FEAST OF THE IMMACULATE CONCEPTION.

1 O Mother! I could weep for mirth,
    Joy fills my heart so fast;
  My soul to-day is heaven on earth,
    Oh, could the transport last!
      I think of thee, and what thou art,
        Thy majesty, thy state;
      And I keep singing in my heart,—
        Immaculate! Immaculate!

2 When Jesus looks upon thy face,
    His Heart with rapture glows,
  And in the Church, by His sweet grace,
    Thy blessed worship grows.
      I think of thee, &c.

3 The angels answer with their songs,
    Bright choirs in gleaming rows;
And saints flock round thy feet in throngs,
    And heaven with bliss o'erflows.
      I think of thee, &c.

4 Oh, blessed be the Eternal Son,
    Who joys to call thee Mother,
And lets poor men by sin undone
    For thy sake call Him Brother!
      I think of thee, &c.

5 Immaculate Conception! far
    Above all graces blest!
Thou shinest like a royal star
    On God's Eternal Breast!
      I think of thee, &c.

178. The Patronage of St. Joseph.

1 DEAR Husband of Mary! dear Nurse of her Child!
Life's ways are full weary, the desert is wild;
Bleak sands are all round us, no home can we see;
Sweet Spouse of our Lady! we lean upon thee.

2 For thou to the pilgrim art Father and Guide,
And Jesus and Mary felt safe by thy side;
Ah, blessed Saint Joseph! how safe should I be,
Sweet Spouse of our Lady! if thou wert with me!

3 O blessed Saint Joseph! how great was thy worth!
The one chosen shadow of God upon earth;
The Father of Jesus, ah, then, wilt thou be,
Sweet Spouse of our Lady! a Father to me?

4 Thou hast not forgotten the long dreary road,
  When Mary took turns with thee, bearing thy God ;
  Yet light was that Burden, none lighter could be :
  Sweet Spouse of our Lady! oh, canst thou bear me?

5 A cold thankless heart, and a mean love of ease,
  What weights, blessed Patron ! more galling than these?
  My life, my past life, thy clear vision may see ;
  Sweet Spouse of our Lady! oh, canst thou love me?

6 Ah, give me thy burden to bear for a while ;
  Let me kiss His warm lips and adore His sweet smile ;
  With her Babe in my arms, surely Mary will be,
  Sweet Spouse of our Lady! my pleader with thee!

7 When the treasures of God were unsheltered on earth,
  Safe keeping was found for them both in thy worth ;
  O Father of Jesus! be father to me,
  Sweet Spouse of our Lady! and I will love thee.

8 God chose thee for Jesus and Mary ! wilt thou
  Forgive a poor exile for choosing thee now?
  There is no saint in heaven I worship like thee :
  Sweet Spouse of our Lady ! oh, deign to love me !

---

179. The Memory of the Dead.

1 Oh, it is sweet to think
  Of those that are departed,
  While murmured Aves sink
  To silence tender-hearted ;

While tears that have no pain
   Are tranquilly distilling,
And the dead live again
   In hearts that love is filling!

2 Yet not as in the days
   Of earthly ties we love them;
For they are touched with rays
   From light that is above them:
Another sweetness shines
   Around their well-known features;
God with His glory signs
   His dearly-ransomed creatures.

3 Ah! they are more our own
   Since now they are God's only;
And each one that has gone
   Has left our heart less lonely.
He mourns not seasons fled,
   Who now in Him possesses
Treasures of many dead
   In their dear Lord's caresses.

4 Dear dead! they have become
   Like guardian angels to us;
And distant heaven, like home,
   Through them begins to woo us,
Love that was earthly wings
   Its flight to holier places;
The dead are sacred things
   That multiply our graces.

5 They whom we loved on earth
   Attract us now to heaven;
Who shared our grief and mirth
   Back to us now are given.
They move with noiseless foot
   Gravely and sweetly round us,
And their soft touch hath cut
   Full many a chain that bound us.

6 O dearest dead! to heaven
 With grudging sighs we gave you,
To Him—be doubts forgiven—
 Who took you there to save you:—
Now get us grace to love
 Your memories yet more kindly;
Pine for our homes above,
 And trust to God more blindly.

180.   Paradise.

1 O Paradise! O Paradise!
 Who doth not crave for rest?
Who would not seek the happy land,
 Where they that loved are blest.
  Where loyal hearts, and true,
  Stand ever in the light,
  All rapture through and through,
  In God's most holy sight?

2 O Paradise! O Paradise!
 The world is growing old;
Who would not be at rest and free
 Where love is never cold?
  Where loyal hearts, &c.

3 O Paradise! O Paradise!
 Wherefore doth death delay,—
Bright death, that is the welcome dawn
 Of our eternal day;
  Where loyal hearts, &c.

4 O Paradise! O Paradise!
 'Tis weary waiting here;
I long to be where Jesus is,
 To feel, to see Him near.

5 O Paradise! O Paradise!
 I want to sin no more;
I want to be as pure on earth
 As on thy spotless shore.
  Where loyal hearts, &c.

6 O Paradise! O Paradise!
 I greatly long to see
The special place my dearest Lord
 Is furnishing for me.
  Where loyal hearts, &c.

7 O Paradise! O Paradise!
 I feel 'twill not be long;
Patience! I almost think I hear
 Faint fragments of thy song.
  Where loyal hearts, &c.

---

181.   Christmas Night.

1 At last Thou art come, little Saviour!
 And Thine angels fill midnight with song;—
Thou art come to us, gentle Creator,
 Whom Thy creatures have sighed for so long!
Chorus.—All hail, Eternal Child!
  Dear Mary's little Flower,
  God, hardly born an hour,
  Sweet Babe of Bethlehem!
  Hail, Mary's Little One!
  Hail, God's Eternal Son!
  Sweet Babe of Bethlehem!
  Sweet Babe of Bethlehem!

2 Thou art come to Thy beautiful Mother!—
 She hath looked on Thy marvellous face;
Thou art come to us, Maker of Mary!
 And she was Thy channel of grace.
  All hail, &c.

3 Thou hast brought with thee plentiful pardon,
    And our souls overflow with delight;
  Our hearts are half broken, dear Jesus!
    With the joy of this wonderful night.
      All hail, &c.

4 We have waited so long for Thee, Saviour!
    Art Thou come to us, dearest, at last?
  Oh, bless Thee, dear joy of Thy Mother!
    This is worth all the wearisome past.
      All hail, &c.

5 Thou art come, Thou art come, Child of Mary!—
    Yet we hardly believe Thou art come;—
  It seems such a wonder to have Thee,
    New Brother! with us in our home.
      All hail, &c.

6 Thou wilt stay with us, Master and Maker!
    Thou wilt stay with us now evermore;
  We will play with Thee, beautiful Brother,
    On eternity's jubilant shore!
      All hail, &c.

INDEX.

	No.
An exile for the Faith	115
Again the Sunday morn	133
All hail, O Lady of the world	59
All hail, dear Conqueror! all hail	94
At the cross her station keeping	33
At last Thou art come, little Saviour	181
All ye who seek in hope and love	21
All ye who seek a certain cure	24
Blest Guardian of all virgin souls	75
Blest is the Faith, divine and strong	152
Christ the Lord is ris'n	92
Christian soul, dost thou desire	147
Christ has two Parents	11
Christians, to the war	153
Come, darkness, spread o'er heaven	32
Come, Holy Ghost, Creator, come	4
Come, Holy Spirit! from the height	5
Come, Holy Ghost, Thy grace inspire	99
Creator of the starry frame	80
Daily, daily, sing to Mary	63
Daughter of Sion! cease thy bitter tears	37
Daughters of Sion! royal maids	41
Day breaks on temple-roofs	50
Day of wrath! the heart dismaying	166
Dear Angel! ever at my side	109
Dear Little One! how sweet Thou art	175
Dear Husband of Mary	178
Eternal glory of the heav'ns	13
Faith of our Fathers! living still	149
Faith of our Fathers! living still (for Ireland)	150
Father of lights! one glance of Thine	117

	No.
Forth comes the Standard of the King	40
Forth let the long procession stream	44
From Sinai's trembling peak	123
God of Mercy! let us run	53
Grace increate	100
Hail, bright Star of ocean	67
Hail, bright Archangel	106
Hail, dread Paternity	12
Hail, Gabriel! hail	107
Hail! holy Joseph, hail	116
Hail, Jesus! hail	27
Hail, Mary, only sinless child	56
Hail, Queen of Heaven	66
Hail, Spear and Nails	42
Hail, Thou living Bread	17
Hail to Thee, true Body	20
Hail to thee, blessed Rood	161
Hail, Virgin-flower	60
Hail, Wounds! which through eternal years	46
Hail, glorious St. Patrick, dear saint of our isle	173
Have mercy on us, God Most High	8
Hark! an awful voice	79
Hark, hark, my soul	151
He who once in righteous vengeance	45
Help, Lord, the souls	165
Holy Ghost, come down upon thy children	6
Holy Mother! pierce me through	84
Holy Spirit, Lord of light	103
I love, I love Thee, Lord most high	159
I love Thee, O my God, my Lord	162
It is my sweetest comfort, Lord	10
It is no earthly summer's ray	112
I rise from dreams of time	174
I was wandering and weary	139
Jesus and Mary! sounds the sweetest	77
Jesu, brightness of the Father	108
Jesu, Creator of the world	23
Jesus! ever-loving Saviour	164
Jesus, my Saviour, my God, my Friend	115
Jesus! my Lord, my God, my All	

	No.
Jesu! the very thought of Thee	25
Jesu, Redeemer of the world	81
Jesus, gentlest Saviour.	176
Jesu! Thy priests' eternal prize	124
Jesu, to Thee we look	140
Jerusalem, thou city blest	131
Joy! joy! the Mother comes	52
Lead us, great teacher Paul	111
Let Alverna's holy mountain	119
Life eternal! life eternal	171
Like the dawning of the morning	51
Look down, O Mother Mary	65
Martyr of unconquer'd might	126
Mother of Mercy! day by day	55
Mother of Christ! hear thou thy people's cry	47
Mother of our Lord and Saviour	64
My God, how wonderful Thou art	1
My God, I love Thee, not because	160
My Jesus, say what wretch has dared	169
None of all the noblest cities	85
Not, Lord, by any will of mine	146
Now at the Lamb's high royal feast	90
Now doth the fiery sun decline	135
Now doth the sun ascend the sky	155
Now let the earth with joy resound	121
Now, while before your relics	138
Now with the fast departing light	158
Now with the slow revolving year	87
O blest Creator of the light	134
O child of God, remember	137
O Christ, Thy guilty people spare	132
Oh, come and mourn with me	29
O cruel Herod	84
O'erwhelmed in depths of woe	39
O Father, Son, and Holy Ghost	168
Oft, my soul, thyself remind	145
O Gift of gifts	142
O Godhead hid	19
O heavenly Jerusalem	172
Oh, turn to Jesus, Mother, turn	62

	No.
Oh, wouldst thou learn, poor self	144
O Jesus Christ, remember	18
O Jesus! God and Man	163
O Jesus, Jesus! dearest Lord	3
O Jesu, my beloved King	143
O Lord, behold a sinner	141
O Lord of perfect purity	156
O mighty Mother	101
O purest of Creatures	48
O Sion! open wide thy gates	73
O soul of Jesus, sick to death	28
O Thou eternal King, most high	95
O Thou immortal Light divine	7
O Thou, in whom my love doth find	96
O Thou, pure light of souls	97
O Thou, th' eternal Father's Word	125
O Thou, the Heaven's eternal King	91
O Thou, the Martyrs glorious King	128
O Thou Thy Mother's Maker, hail	130
O Thou the Father's Image blest	136
O Thou, who Thine own Father's breast	78
Oh, it is sweet to think	179
O Paradise! O Paradise	180
O vision bright	57
O Mother! I could weep for mirth	177
O God! Thy power is wonderful	2
Peter, blest Shepherd	110
Saint of the Sacred Heart	113
See, amid the winter snow	83
See from on high	86
See! where in shame the God of glory hangs	88
Signed with the cross	167
Sing, my tongue, the Saviour's glory	88
Sing, my tongue, the Saviour's glory	105
Sing, O earth, for thy redemption	14
Sing, sing, ye Angel Bands	54
Sing we the Martyrs blest	127
Sion, lift thy voice, and sing	104
Sleep, holy Babe	20
Son of the Highest! deign to cast	11

	No.
Soon the fiery sun ascending	15
Soul of Jesus, make me holy	170
Sovereign Will enthroned on high	9
Spotless Anna! Juda's glory	68
Star of Jacob, ever beaming	58
St. Francis kneels at Rome	120
Sweet Morn! thou Parent	69
Sweet Saviour! bless us	154
The Angel spake the word	70
The day, the happy day, is dawning	49
The Lord's eternal gifts	122
The life which God's Incarnate Word	114
The moon is in the heavens	61
The Saviour left high heaven to dwell	74
The sun is sinking fast	157
The Word, descending	22
This day the wond'rous mystery	43
This is the image of the Queen	76
Thou Crown of all the Virgin choir	129
Thou loving Maker of mankind	86
Thousands of years had come and gone	30
Thus did Christ to perfect manhood	89
Virgin of all virgins best	35
What a sea of tears and sorrow	31
What mortal tongue can sing thy praise	71
When the Patriarch was returning	16
Whither thus, in holy rapture	72
Why is thy face so lit with smiles	98
Ye faithful, approach ye	82
Ye sons and daughters of the Lord	93

Te Deum laudamus.

Te Deum laudámus: * te Dóminum confitémur.

Te ætérnum Patrem * omnis terra venerátur.

Tibi omnes angeli, * tibi cœli, et univérsæ potestátes:

Tibi chérubim et séraphim, * incessábili voce proclámant:

Sanctus, sanctus, sanctus, * Dóminus Deus Sábaoth:

Pleni sunt cœli et terra, * majestátis glóriæ tuæ.

Te gloriósus * Apostolórum chorus.

Te Prophetárum * laudábilis númerus.

Te Mártyrum candidátus * laudat exércitus.

Te per orbem terrárum * sancta confitétur Ecclésia.

Patrem * imménsæ majestátis.

Venerándum tuum verum * et únicum Filium

We praise thee, O God: we acknowledge thee to be the Lord.

All the earth doth worship thee: the Father everlasting.

To thee all angels cry aloud: the heavens and all the powers therein:

To thee cherubim and seraphim: continually do cry:

Holy, holy, holy: Lord God of Sabaoth.

Heaven and earth are full: of the majesty of thy glory.

The glorious choir of the Apostles: praise thee.

The admirable company of the Prophets: praise thee.

The white-robed army of Martyrs: praise thee.

The Holy Church throughout all the world: doth acknowledge thee.

The Father: of an infinite majesty.

Thy adorable, true and only Son.

Sanctum quoque * Paráclitum Spíritum.

Tu Rex glóriæ,* Christe.

Tu Patris * sempitérnus es Fílius.

Tu ad liberándum susceptúrus hóminem, * non horruísti Vírginis úterum.

Tu devícto mortis acúleo, * aperuísti credéntibus regna cœlórum.

Tu ad déxteram Dei sedes, * in glória Patris.

Judex créderis * esse ventúrus.

¹ Te ergo quæsumus, tuis fámulis súbveni, * quos pretióso sánguine redemísti.

Ætérna fac cum Sanctis tuis, * in glória numerári.

Salvum fac pópulum tuum, Domine, * et bénedic hæreditáti tuæ.

Et rege eos, et extólle illos, * usque in ætérnum.

Per singulos dies * benedícimus te.

Et laudámus nomen tu-

Also the Holy Ghost : the Comforter.

Thou art the King of Glory : O Christ.

Thou art the everlasting Son : of the Father.

When thou tookest upon thee to deliver man : thou didst not abhor the Virgin's womb.

When thou hadst overcome the sting of death : thou didst open the kingdom of heaven to all believers.

Thou sittest at the right hand of God : in the glory of the Father.

We believe that thou shalt come : to be our Judge.

We pray thee, therefore, help thy servants : whom thou hast redeemed with thy precious blood.

Make them to be numbered with thy Saints : in glory everlasting.

O Lord, save thy people : and bless thine inheritance.

Govern them : and lift them up for ever.

Day by day : we magnify thee.

And we praise thy name

---

¹ Here it is usual to kneel.

um in sæculum, * et in sæculum sæculi.

Dignáre, Dómine, die isto,* sine peccáto nos custodíre.

Miserére nostri, Dómine, * miserére nostri.

Fiat misericórdia tua, Dómine, super nos : * quemádmodum sperávimus in te.

In te, Dómine, sperávi; * non confúndar in ætérnum.

for ever : yea, for ever and ever.

Vouchsafe, O Lord, this day : to keep us without sin.

O Lord, have mercy upon us : have mercy upon us.

O Lord, let thy mercy be shewed upon us : as we have hoped in thee.

O Lord, in thee have I hoped : let me not be confounded for ever.

On occasions of Thanksgiving the following are added:

℣. Benedictus es, Domine, Deus Patrum nostrorum.

℟. Et laudabilis, et gloriosus in sæcula.

℣. Benedicamus Patrem et Filium, cum Sancto Spiritu.

℟. Laudemus et superexaltemus eum in sæcula.

℣. Benedictus es, Domine Deus, in firmamento cœli.

℟. Et laudabilis, et gloriosus, et superexaltatus in sæcula.

℣. Benedic, anima mea, Dominum.

℟. Et noli oblivisci retributiones ejus.

℣. Domine, exaudi orationem meam.

℟. Et clamor meus ad te veniat.

℣. Dominus vobiscum.

℟. Et cum spiritu tuo.

Oremus.

Deus, cujus misericordiæ non est numerus, et bonitatis

℣. Blessed art thou, O Lord, the God of our fathers.

℟. And worthy to be praised, and glorious for ever.

℣. Let us bless the Father and the Son, with the Holy Ghost.

℟. Let us praise and magnify him for ever.

℣. Blessed art thou, O Lord, in the firmament of heaven.

℟. And worthy to be praised, glorious and exalted for ever.

℣. Bless the Lord, O my soul.

℟. And forget not all his benefits.

℣. O Lord, hear my prayer.

℟. And let my cry come unto thee.

℣. The Lord be with you.

℟. And with thy spirit.

Let us pray.

O God, whose mercies are without number, and the trea-

infinitus est thesaurus piissimæ majestati tuæ pro collatis donis gratias agimus, tuam semper clementiam exorantes: ut qui petentibus postulata concedis, eosdem non deserens, ad præmia futura disponas.

Deus, qui corda fidelium Sancti Spiritus illustratione docuisti: da nobis in eodem Spiritu recta sapere, et de ejus semper consolatione gaudere.

Deus, qui neminem in te sperantem nimium affligi permittis, sed pium precibus præstas auditum: pro postulationibus nostris, votisque susceptis gratias agimus, te piissime deprecantes, ut a cunctis semper muniamur adversis. Per Christum Dominum nostrum.

℞. Amen.

sure of whose goodness is infinite: we render thanks to th[e] most gracious Majesty for th[e] gifts thou hast bestowed upo[n] us, evermore beseeching th[y] clemency: that as thou gran[t]est the petitions of them th[at] ask thee, thou wilt never fo[r]sake them, but wilt prepa[re] them for the rewards to come.

O God, who hast taught th[e] hearts of the faithful by th[e] light of the Holy Spirit: gra[nt] us, by the same Spirit, to r[e]lish what is right, and eve[r] more to rejoice in his consola tion.

O God, who sufferest non[e] that hope in thee to be afflicte[d] over much, but dost afford a gra[-] cious ear unto their prayers we render thee thanks for tha[t] thou hast heard our supplica tions and vows; and we mo[st] humbly beseech thee, that w[e] may evermore be protected fro[m] all adversities. Through Chris[t] our Lord.

℞. Amen.

www.ingramcontent.com/pod-product-compliance
Lightning Source LLC
Chambersburg PA
CBHW030820190426
43197CB00036B/686